CiDER REVOLUTiON!

YOUR DiY GUiDE TO CiDER & PÉT-NAT

MiKAEL NYPELiUS & KARL SJÖSTRÖM

PAVILION

CONTENTS

FRUIT iN STEREO

Every autumn in Sweden, we're left with an abundance of surplus fruit in domestic gardens and old orchards. What a waste, we thought, and started our revolution. With simple equipment and an open mindset anyone can make exciting fermented fruit drinks using apples, pears, plums and berries.

Our revolution is anchored in the belief that our fruit is worth celebrating. For us, nothing is off limits and the traditional boundaries between cider, beer and wine are no longer relevant. With a bit of creativity, attentiveness to nature and a little knowledge about natural fermentation processes, you can produce drinks with honest flavours and great complexity, without using any ingredients other than those you've picked yourself. By drawing on insights from beer brewers and winemakers, we want to show you how you can ferment small- and medium-sized batches that will truly do justice to the fruit.

The idea behind Fruktstereo is to celebrate Swedish fruit, but when we started reading about traditional cidermaking it became clear that Sweden isn't thought to have any 'real' cider apples that have the bitterness and character of apples from other European cider nations. Our classic cooking apples are sweet, tasty and tart. Perhaps there wasn't any future in making real good cider up here in the north?

But, with a firm belief that super tasty apples picked straight from the tree should be able to be fermented into a really tasty drink, we employed all our combined experience from the wine world. We embarked on a journey towards a new type of Scandinavian cider – very different from the French, English or Spanish varieties. A unique beverage for our climate and our fruit, in a style that we want to drink ourselves. By mixing in other fruits and berries we might veer away from what many consider cider to be, but why should that matter?

Long live the cider revolution!

Karl and Mikael

WHAT IS CIDER

The question 'What is cider?' might seem straightforward – most people will simply think of an alcoholic apple beverage. But there's far more to cider than that. The flavour can be anything from super sweet to bone dry, from mega bitter to easy drinking, the alcohol content almost zero or with a proper bite to it. It's not just apples: other fruits and berries come into play, and, there is also a lot of variation in the fruit-juice content of different ciders.

Sweden has produced cider since time immemorial, but industrial production has been dominant since the 1950s. Sweden can hardly be regarded as being an influential cider country internationally. If you ask people what characterizes Swedish cider, 'sweet alcoholic soda pop' is likely to be a common verdict. However, this type of cider is found in many places around the world although it is indeed often known as 'Swedish cider'.

In Europe, the regulations for what can be called cider vary from country to country, but the Swedish style is based on the definition from the Swedish Food Agency: 'Cider is a beverage that is produced from fermented fruit juice from apples and/or pears... The fruit juice content in the finished product should be at least 15% by volume.' This is something we think should be highlighted. Do consumers know that the drinks in this category only have to contain 15% fruit juice? That's a completely different cider compared with a product that contains 100% fruit juice. To draw a comparison with the wine world: it is a given that a bottle of wine contains 100% grapes – imagine the scandal if the producers started to dilute the wine with other fermentable juice, or even water. But within cidermaking it is clearly regarded as completely normal.

Around the world

British cider has a long history. In legal terms it needs a minimum of 35% apple or pear juice, although the 'real cider' movement requires at least 90% fresh pressed juice. One traditional style is firmly rooted in the countryside of the west of England and is mainly produced as still, dry 'farmhouse' cider (so-called scrumpy). This can often be fairly bitter since it's made from traditional cider apples that are high in tannins. A range of different cider styles are also produced here, and the bitter character can be tempered by retaining some of the natural sugars in a process called keeving.

Keeving is a method that aims to 'invert' the yeast, so that it sits on the top instead of sinking to the bottom, usually by adding enzymes. This way you can easily rack the cider from the yeast. Moreover, it's common to filter the cider through a microfilter to make sure it's as clean as possible when bottling. Executed correctly, keeving will slow down the fermentation and eventually stop it – before all the sugar has converted into alcohol. This leaves a certain amount of sweetness, with a small amount of bubbles. In eastern parts of England, cider is traditionally made using dessert apples and is therefore lighter and less rustic in character.

French cider, with a bitter bite, oxidized tones from over-ripe fruit and often with some residual sweetness, is another style often associated with artisan cider. Thanks to the keeving method, which is very common in Brittany and Normandy, the cider, which would otherwise be regarded as far too bitter and dry, becomes a bit more balanced. There's an almost infinite number of fruit trees and different apple and pear varieties in these regions and it's therefore common to classify these cider apples into a few main groups to get a better overview: bittersweet, bitter, acidic and sweet. To achieve a good balance to the cider, the different varieties are blended. Moreover, the fruit often comes from old trees, sometimes several hundred years old. If it's picked too early, the fruit is inedible, the bitterness is enormously high and the cider not very drinkable. If you wait until the fruit is thoroughly ripe, or has fallen from the tree, the bitterness is muted and will also add an oxidized note to the cider. A fairly large amount of cider is also produced in south-west France, where it is similar to the cider on the other side of the border in northern Spain, since the climate and apple varieties are more or less the same.

10

One of our musical homages, in this case to Oasis' classic 'Definitely Maybe'.

In France, cider must be made from 100% apple juice. It is labelled doux (sweet), demi-sec (medium) or brut (dry). The sweet ciders are low in alcohol because less sugar has been converted during the fermentation. Any of the styles may be still or naturally sparkling (cidre bouché) after a second fermentation in the bottle.

Spain also has a long tradition of cidermaking. There, apple trees have grown wild, and later been cultivated, for hundreds of years. In Asturias, cider is called sidra and in the Basque country it's called sagardoa. Just as in other well-known cider regions, the apple varieties grow well in the cool and wet climate and develop their flavours and aromas during long growing seasons. Asturias produces more cider than any other part of Spain and just like in Normandy there is a more developed regulatory framework when it comes to fruit varieties and production methods in comparison with other regions. The style is often still, acidic and completely dry. Traditionally it is fermented and aged in large wooden barrels that are often made from chestnut. This creates a so-called reductive style and the cider might therefore need 'airing'.

Reduction and a reductive style can be characterized by something being absent – the beverage can feel restrained and perhaps a bit shy. It can also smell slightly of 'fart', something that indicates that the beverage needs decanting, that is, the beverage needs pouring over into a carafe. In Asturias, this aeration is achieved by holding the bottle high and pouring the cider in a long stream down into the glass. This accentuates the fruit in the beverage and also tones down the acidity.

In the USA, all types of beverages made from apples and/or pears are called cider. Juice and fermented juice is called hard cider. In Sweden, in the past all kinds of fruit beverages made from apples and pears were called 'must', with or without alcohol.

Cider our way

At Fruktstereo our understanding of the regulations around cider has been somewhat patchy.

This was proven when we gleefully and euphorically made almost 10,000 litres (2,200 gallons) of 'cider' according to the Swedish definition but using press leftovers from our actual cidermaking. We managed to get it just under 3.5% ABV and thought we could sell the cider in supermarkets, in the same way as lower-alcohol beer. Just as we were about to launch it, we were made aware of the fact that cider stronger than 2.25% ABV is not permitted to be sold in standard shops. Although our product, in our view, is considerably better, and certainly more honest, than most other ciders on the market it seems that the contents of a bottle are less important than sticking to the rules.

Regulations state that cider should be made from apples and/ or pears. We think this is odd, since other readily accessible fruit contain sugar and flavours that can give an exciting character to cider.

So, what is real cider according to us? In our cider revolution, cider is a naturally fermented fruit drink without any additives, made from 100% fruit.

Of course, this opens up more questions: Why is a fermented drink made from grapes called wine, while a drink fermented from apples or pears is called cider? And why do you get a fruit wine if the drink is still, or made from fruit other than grapes? Since when did grapes become something else other than fruit? More and more questions are popping up the more we work on this, but we keep on fermenting and focus on the finished drink without letting definitions get in the way.

When we first started talking about making real Swedish cider, the idea was first to try to achieve a style that was fully fermented and dry, similar to cider from Normandy and Brittany in France, for example. But when we started reading into how they make cider in those regions it was always pointed out that it was the special cider apples that contributed the bitterness and complexity required to make a good 'adult cider'. We could have given up there and then. Our classic Swedish apple varieties 'only' contribute a good fruitiness and acidity. But something made us embark on our first tentative experiments regardless.

The results were surprising. Despite our Swedish apples, the cider became complex and expressive – even without any European cider apples! Of course, the cider turned out completely different to any we'd tried before, more acidic and fresher than classic French and British cider, but in our opinion at least as complex and interesting. It probably wasn't the French or British semi-dry and fairly bitter cider that we would have preferred to drink. The fresh and sprightly style we started to find reminded us more of the wines that we happily sat and analysed together with friends until the early hours whenever we got the chance. The same friends praised our first cider attempts but couldn't understand how this hadn't been made sooner in Sweden or Scandinavia.

Natural wine FTW!

In order to understand our thought process when we make our drinks, we should explain our affinity with the movement of winemakers and wine drinkers that are linked by the, not entirely clear, definition 'natural wine'. It's a movement with roots in 1980s France, where a group of wine growers and enthusiasts tirelessly campaigned for grapes to be cultivated without any pesticides and the wine produced without any additives, in a way that was as natural as possible. At the other end of the spectrum are the conventional wines made from grapes sprayed with pesticides and produced to a 'recipe'. With varying amounts of sulphur, sugar, enzymes and a range of other ways to manipulate the finished drink, the result will often become something entirely unrecognizable that we would not call wine.

To develop as much character as possible from the grapes, winemakers with a natural focus will use simple but controlled techniques. The aim is to create a drink that accentuates where the grapes have come from and their character. Among these winemakers, local grape varieties are the most important, and instead of planting modern varieties, they will look at what has historically been grown locally. Those varieties have been proven to thrive in the local climate and soil. Exactly how these factors affect the wine is usually called the wine's, or perhaps primarily, the grape's, 'terroir'. Terroir is, in wine circles, an almost mythical concept that includes everything that can have an impact on the grapes as they grow and which means that a specific grape

14

variety can differ significantly from the same variety grown in a different place.

Even when grapes grow in a specific terroir, their character can easily be lost during the production of the wine. Without a continued natural approach, wines are often streamlined to match taste preferences within a specific target audience. Loads of added sulphur, enzymes and various types of laboratory-grown yeast are not the terroir's best friend. And this is just a tiny part of everything you're allowed to add to wine and other drinks nowadays.

Just as old vines create more complexity and concentration in wines than newly planted ones, older fruit trees will grow fruit with more character. When we started picking fruit from abandoned orchards, we were very surprised by what they could offer in terms of complexity and diversity – it was just as it is with grapes!

The fruit above all

We quickly came to the following conclusion: in cidermaking, just as in winemaking, the ingredients are at the heart of everything. If you've got good fruit, you will have the prerequisites to make really good cider. But it's not everything. If you adopt certain approaches from winemaking and beer brewing, you can steer the result of your fermented fruit in any direction. From winemaking we have adopted the methods of how to treat the juice and the leftovers from the crushing, through maceration for example (which you can read more about on page 58), and how you can blend juice from different varieties and types of fruit to develop the desired character (read more about how we blend on page 60). It's also from the wine world (and nowadays the worlds of coffee and beer) that we have taken the vocabulary to evaluate and analyse the experience of a cider. Many of our references in regard to the type of flavours we like and want to accentuate, can be found in the natural wine world, as well as a lot of the general philosophy that we are working towards.

The beer-brewing culture has also exploded in the last couple of decades. All of a sudden there is an almost infinite number of microbreweries challenging the rules that the large breweries have traditionally adhered to. We can take a lot of inspiration from how bold modern beer-brewers are when it comes to new recipes, flavours and collaborations. There are no taboos and even doing something 'wrong' can be rewarded by becoming a trend, if the error establishes a new technique.

An important difference between brewing beer and making cider our way is that we believe that the fruit's natural yeasts will give the best result. Therefore, we don't add commercial yeast at any stage, but put our faith in the yeast that already exists on the fruit's skin. You can read more about how the yeast will affect the result on page 51. Using the fruit's own yeast means that your cider can take a considerable time to make, so the whole process requires patience. In some cases, several years of bottle ageing may be required to achieve the desired result.

OUR PROCESS

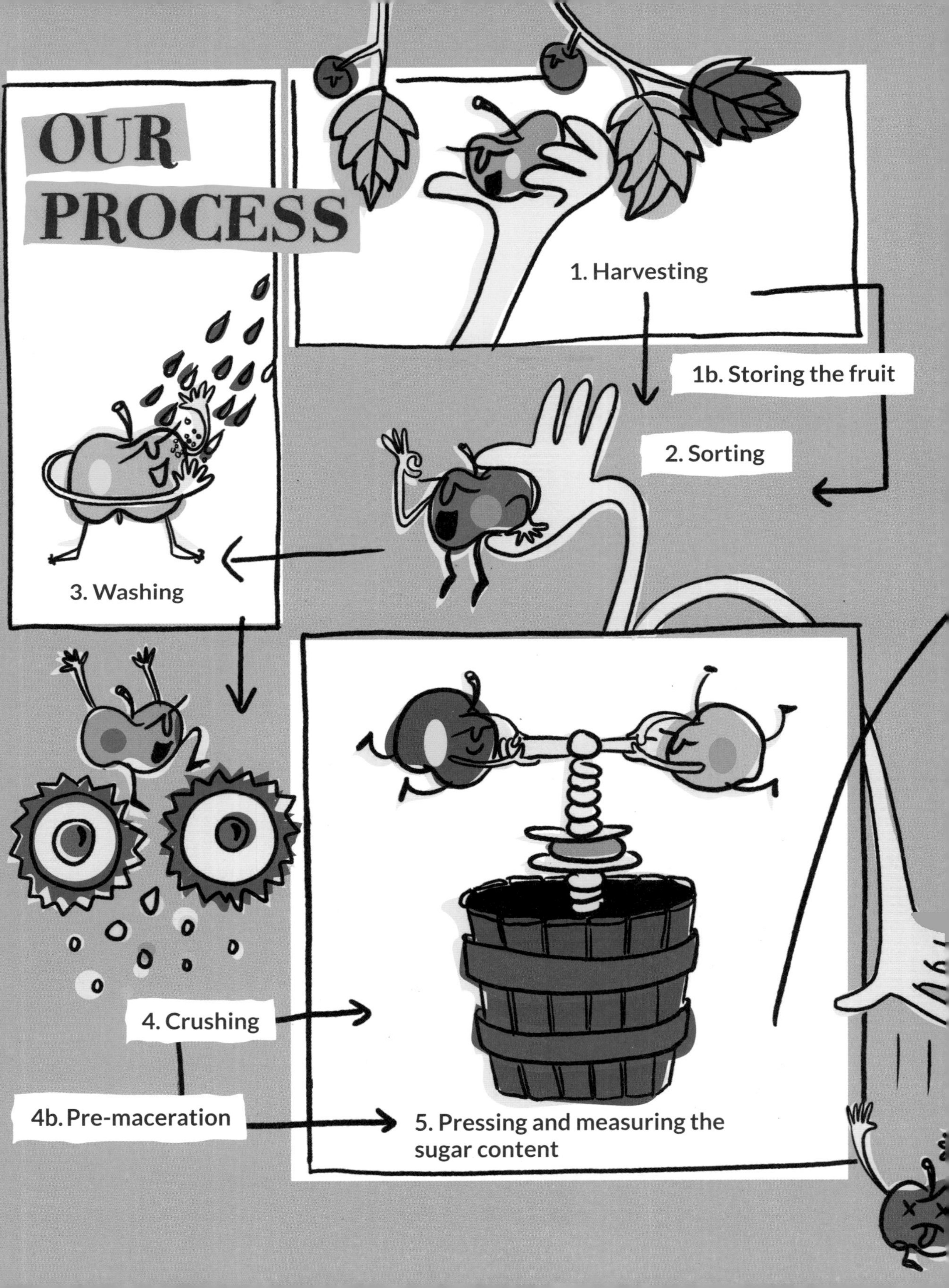

1. Harvesting

1b. Storing the fruit

2. Sorting

3. Washing

18

4. Crushing

4b. Pre-maceration

5. Pressing and measuring the sugar content

6b. Post-maceration

6. Fermenting, racking, measuring the sugar content

9b. Disgorging

19

7. Blending

8. Bottling

9. Bottle fermenting and ageing

HARVE

Since we don't have any plantings of our own, we spend a lot of time driving around, mostly in Skåne and on Gotland, eagerly looking out for fruit trees. The autumn is the most exciting time but it's also the most stressful. Make sure you have a few autumn weekends earmarked for picking!

STING

Every time we pass a garden or a tree out in the wild, we start thinking about a possible harvest. Our adrenaline levels increase and plans for when and how to harvest these particular trees start to form. If it's getting towards the end of the harvest season, it can mean that other activities get postponed. Our families and friends are used to us suddenly disappearing off to harvest fruit that can't wait.

Over time, individuals with surplus garden fruit, or with large neglected farms or orchards, have started to get in touch to ask if we can take care of their fruit. This means that autumns are all about gathering a big gang of people who are up for picking fruit with us. It's always stressful trying to pick as much fruit as possible before it's too late.

Since the trees we pick from tend to not have been pruned or treated in any way for a very long time, we can hardly call them cultivated fruit trees. Instead, we usually say that we pick from 'planted trees'. That is, they might have been pruned and looked after at some stage and then left to grow naturally. This means that many of the trees we pick from have grown large and rampant, with long offshoots and also a lot of branches that are partly or completely dead and that have moss and other things growing on them. This will understandably reduce the tree's capacity to produce large quantities of fruit, since the aim with pruning, among other things, is to expose more parts of the tree to sunlight, which will yield more fruit.

The trees are our heroes

When a tree is allowed to grow naturally and interact with its environment, it will create a microclimate with loads of different plants and animals living together. We think that this naturally created cycle is fantastic in many ways. Above all, it will give a higher minerality and concentration: when the tree roots are finding their way deep down into the living soil, ionic minerals can be transferred to the fruit. But there are also other flavour characteristics that are different in comparison with fruit from trees that are cultivated for production with a focus on quantity. Those flavour characteristics can be expressed in words such as wilder, more alive, or as we usually summarize it – with more energy. The energy in the fruit and in the finished drink is something we will come back to.

The age of the tree also has a role to play. Younger specimens can yield a lot of fruit, but the complexity of the flavours will develop with age, just as with older grape vines. Older trees will yield a smaller crop and eventually will also lose their youthful strength, but what you get is concentration and other types of energy – flavour vibrations that are more complex and longer, more intensive and from deeper within the soil and the plants. The abandoned trees that we pick from, which may be more than 100 years old, are also fantastic just to look at. It's almost as if they have their own personalities. We get to know the trees as we pick from them and hope eventually to be able to look after them so that they will survive and give us fruit for a long time to come. We shouldn't forget all the old trees that deserve our appreciation.

Old orchards and farms are also the places where we often find multiple varieties of fruit. Today's fruit producers grow fewer varieties than before and only cultivate varieties that are nice to eat straight away or that can be stored for a long time. That said, we absolutely don't demand fruit that is specifically intended for cidermaking – but it would be nice if there wasn't such a focus on only growing one or two varieties of dessert apples with simple character and flavour, but instead on some of the hundreds of cooking apples or late-season dessert apples that used to be grown in Sweden and that can still occasionally be found in gardens and old orchards.

Finding fruit

If you don't have a garden, or a friend with a garden, our tip is to simply knock on the door of someone who has fruit trees. Check if the person owns the garden and was intending on using the fruit for eating, cooking, making jam, marmalade or juice – and if not, perhaps they would consider donating some of it to you instead of letting it go to waste. Fermented fruit drinks are a good cause, after all, and perhaps you can promise a bottle in return. Maybe you can even get some currants, rhubarb or other useful fruit while you're there. If the person in question was intending on using their fruit themselves, that is also good news, and in that case, a future exchange of knowledge would be the worst thing to come from the door knocking.

There are also fruit trees that grow wild and in public spaces. A trick is to start looking for trees early on in the season, perhaps during spring when they're in bloom, and mark the likely contenders out on a map on your phone. Then you will be prepared once the fruit starts to ripen and fall off the trees.

Surplus from cultivation

We have also noticed that our commercial fruit producers often have an enormous amount of surplus fruit. In bad years, a lot of the fruit will be sorted out because it's the wrong size, has frost damage or other minor defects which means it can't be sold. Good years can mean a surplus of sellable fruit that they can't cope with. Nowadays, the same applies for some grape producers in southern Sweden, who in good fruit years will have so many grapes that they aren't able to process them all in time. In the case of grapes, it's much more important to process them just after harvesting than it is for apples.

28

Picking

Picking fruit is probably the easiest and most enjoyable task in the world, or at least in the cider world. Get outside on a sunny day and pick the fruit that would otherwise have gone to waste. For us, the timing of the harvest is down to how the fruit is tasting, but also when we have time to take care of it.

Of course, hand picking directly from the branch is the best way to keep the fruit as clean as possible and to avoid dents and bruises. Some people say that you should handle the fruit as carefully as you would an egg, but for us it depends on when you will press it. You can be fairly heavy-handed if you are picking fruit that has the right level of ripeness and that you will press straight away. If the trees are large, hand picking will be too tedious and difficult. In that case you will have to shake down the fruit by climbing up to the crown of the tree or use a technique that looks like an aggressive take on tree hugging. This is very efficient and will also give you a good workout after a couple of large trunks. Shaking the tree and then picking the fruit from the ground is efficient, since many of the trees we harvest have grown rampant, with a lot of the fruit sitting high up in the crown. This technique is preferable for most garden trees, since you don't have to climb trees or ladders. With a large tarpaulin or net underneath the crown, the fruit can be picked up quickly and easily and you will avoid getting them unnecessarily dirty. The tarp will also act as a shock absorber, giving the fruit a softer landing.

The right ripeness

If we are pressing straight away, we prefer the apples to be as ripe as possible: this will give the highest level of concentration, sugar content, aromatic notes and natural yeast strains. It also means that the fermentation will usually get going quickly. If, on the other hand, you pick over-ripe fruit, or leave the fruit in storage for too long, it will be difficult to crush and press with a good result, mainly because the structure of the fruit will have broken down too much. The result will be a fruit mush that is difficult to juice (but if you can be bothered, over-ripe fruit can give fantastic tropical notes from Swedish fruit).

If the fruit on the tree already has a good flavour balance, it's sensible to process it fairly soon after picking. If it is still too acidic, you can leave it on the tree for longer, or pick it and store it for a while and then taste it again in a couple of weeks.

The late summer berries and early apple and pear varieties together with the proper late autumn and winter apples, create a very long season, with a lot of variety in flavour and character. With everything from sweet, neutral and fruitier varieties such as Aroma, Ingrid Marie and Cox's Orange Pippin to acidic, aromatic and complex varieties such as Belle de Boskoop and Ribston Pippin, you can make drinks with different methods and processes during a large part of the year.

We have of course got a few favourite varieties that have more structure and that give a more interesting expression to the finished cider. However, there is no reason why you should limit yourself – our gut feeling is that almost all apple varieties as well as other fruit can be used, depending on what cider style you want to make, and which processes you choose. In order to decide on the process, duration of maceration and so on, we taste the fruit straight from the tree. This is one of the most satisfying moments during the cidermaker's year – to bite into a fruit that has grown for half a year and developed all the elements that are necessary to hopefully make a good cider.

Time for pears
Some fruit will need picking at exactly the right time. Most pear varieties we have in Sweden are eating or cooking varieties and are significantly more sensitive than most apples. They will need picking close to the processing day to bring out the flavours and aromas and to prevent them from getting soft and spoiled. The pears we use are fairly early varieties and we pick them straight from the tree: windfalls will bruise and spoil quickly.

Just as with pears, soft and delicate plums aren't suited for storing. The ripening time for plums that grow on the same tree can vary a lot and they may therefore need picking in several rounds.

Storing fruit

Most of the fruit we work with can be picked over a long period and at different stages of ripeness, and then be stored for anything from a couple of days up to several months. Because the storing time for apples can be very long, we can juice and ferment fruit almost all year round. After harvesting, we store the fruit in small crates made from cardboard, wood or plastic, or in larger boxes that can take 400–500 kg (880–1,100 lb). The advantage with smaller crates is that there won't be as much pressure on the fruit at the bottom. It's good to keep the storing temperature as cold as possible as long as the fruit doesn't freeze.

Apple varieties that are picked later in the year are particularly suited to being stored cold, as they will reach a better ripeness and some of the natural processes inside the fruit will get going. Apples of this type are robust and compact, with a thick, tough skin. Some varieties can even stay on the trees until after the first frost or snow.

To help the fruit keep even longer during storage, harvest it before it has reached its peak ripeness. Since it's not fully ripe, the structure won't have started to break down and it will keep fresh for longer. However, the sugar content and the flavours will not have developed as much as you would want, but the biggest problem is probably that the yeast strains can be too weak to start the fermentation at all.

Suitable places for storing

The humidity shouldn't be too high since mould can start to grow and spoil the fruit. A garage or storehouse that doesn't go below freezing are usually great, or a dry cellar with some air circulation. If you don't have a lot of space for storing, it's better to harvest when most of the fruit is ripe and process it straight away.

For larger scale production there is also low oxygen cold storage, where the fruit can be stored for a very long time without losing any of its original character and structure. Producers will often keep early harvested fruit in this type of storage to be able to sell it in the spring.

To know if a fruit has exactly the right ripeness, you can check the pH value and the sugar content, among other things. For this you will need different types of measuring equipment. Since we think that too much technical equipment and analysis make the production more boring, we have chosen to use our sense of taste and simpler methods instead. Find out a bit more about that later on in the book when we discuss fermentation.

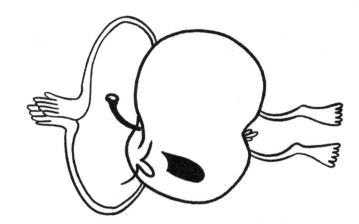

During the long harvest season, we combine fruit picking with work in the cidery, but once autumn has properly arrived and the temperature starts to climb down towards zero, we spend more and more time in the cidery. Now we really begin the work of creating drinks from the fantastic fruit.

JUICING

It's good to have thought through how you will process the fruit before harvesting, since the equipment for juicing needs to be in place. It's not unusual that you will end up with five times as much fruit as you had planned for, so it doesn't hurt to have equipment that is slightly on the generous side.

Regardless of your level of ambition, you will need to wash, crush and press your apples, and you will need a vessel to ferment the juice in.

Make sure you have access to running water so that you can rinse and clean tools and fermentation vessels or vats. To be able to work naturally and without any additives, it's especially important that everything is clean, and that insects and unwelcome bacteria aren't able to contaminate the vats. It's imperative to wash tools before and after every use. Our experience tells us that if the fermentation fails, it's something in these particular steps that has gone wrong. Apart from running the risk of spoiling the cider, failing to keep up good hygiene and cleanliness can also pose a health risk. Remember to wash your hands and avoid touching the inside of the vats with your fingers, especially in the stages when the juice isn't fermenting.

The journal
We keep a simple journal to keep track of what we do. It's sensible since we rarely remember everything that happened during the whole process. For each batch we have a document tracking the picking of the fruit, choice of fruit, crushing, maceration, pressing, fermentation, racking, bottling and sugar content at different stages and sometimes other comments that can be useful to remember. With this information, we can then learn from the different stages and results, and eventually, hopefully, get even better at what we do.

Sorting and washing

The first step in the juicing process is to sort through and discard any bad fruit. This might be fruit damaged in picking or that has spoiled during storage. Not every apple with the slightest blemish has to be discarded. Minor bruising, scab and frost damages won't have a notable effect on the end product as long as the fruit is tasty and otherwise in good condition. The sorting can be carried out at a standard table or in small crates.

After sorting, wash the fruit in a bucket or a plastic tank using a standard garden hose. The idea is to remove any loose particles, in particular soil and dirt that can spoil the end product.

Don't go over the top

In our first year of production, we stood in a cold room and meticulously checked over each fruit to decide whether it was fit for the next stage or not. We suffered, hunkered over in temperatures just above freezing, and pushed apples into buckets of cold water with our bare hands to almost entirely scrub off each and every little spot. What we have learnt since then is not to go over the top with the cleaning. After a few study trips to French cidermakers, it became clear that this particular step wasn't given much importance. After harvesting, they started shovelling fruit directly into the crusher. We asked the owner of an apple farm about washing: he laughed and explained that they do in fact wash the fruit sometimes – whatever they haven't got time to process will remain on open trailers and if it rains, the fruit will get a shower! In other words, a visual sort through of the fruit, followed by light washing, is enough to get a good end result.

Crushing

To be able to press the fruit you will usually have to crush it first. Fruit crushers come in various sizes and models, from hand-turned to electric. Depending on the apple variety or fruit that you are using, you might have to adjust the degree of crushing. Hard fruit might need to be crushed in smaller pieces to be able to extract an adequate amount of juice, while soft fruit might need to be in larger pieces to avoid ending up with a mush that's difficult to press.

The crushed pulp will oxidize and turn brown relatively quickly, just as when you bite into an apple. However, this is nothing to worry about, but a stage that can have a positive effect on the finished cider.

Pre-maceration

The time the crushed fruit pulp is left before pressing we call pre-maceration. Pre-maceration is done to extract aromas and flavours over a short period of time before pressing. This maceration or leaching also makes the fruit easier to press and you will be able to extract more juice due to enzymes that naturally break down the fruit's structure. You can read more about how maceration is used in winemaking on page 127.

The maceration stage is especially interesting for those of us making a new style of cider using Scandinavian apples. Our local apples are mostly dessert apples or cooking apples with high acidity and good natural balance. With these relatively neutral apple varieties you can play around a lot more with maceration times and mixing with other fruit and berries than in many other cider regions. There, the fruit is often pressed straight away due to its high bitterness. When we have tried maceration using the few cider apples or crab apples that we pick, the flavour became way too bitter and heavy on tannins, at least for our palates.

As a general rule, our approach is the following: for a light, fresh and fruity cider the maceration time is short, and for a more complex and darker cider it gets longer. In the recipe section we provide suggestions for maceration times depending on what type of apples you use.

Pressing

Once the fruit has been crushed, the pulp is ready to be pressed in a fruit press of some kind. There is a range of different models; we started off with a small manual basket press, which we show in the step-by-step section. There are basket presses that are powered by electricity, hydro presses with a bladder that are powered solely by water pressure and pneumatic models that are powered by electricity and air pressure. The important thing is that you can extract juice which can then be fermented to make cider. Generally, the higher the pressure used to press the fruit pulp, the more juice and flavours you will get.

However, too high a pressure can extract too many tannins from the skin and core, resulting in an unbalanced cider. Moderation is key, but what moderation is depends on the fruit variety and how hard it is. Our tip is to taste the juice that gets extracted. As long as it's not too bitter, you can continue pressing. Otherwise, it might be time to stop.

If you take an example from the wine world, some producers say a quick direct pressing is the best, while others prefer a slower pressing, for example by using a vertical press, where the fruit pulp's own weight will slowly press out the juice, which can sometimes take several days. This is a step that we will continue to focus on as we get get even better at adjusting the pressing according to the type of fruit and maceration times. Because we believe this is where it's possible to finetune and therefore make even better cider.

Measuring the sugar content

Once you've got your freshly pressed juice, it's time to find out the sugar content. Once you know the sugar content, you can find out the potential alcohol content of the fermented juice and get a rough idea of how long the fermentation will take. Use a simple hydrometer that you'll be able to find in any shop that sells home brewing equipment, or buy a slightly more expensive refractometer which is more exact but can only measure the sugar content before the juice has started to ferment. Various scales are used to measure sugar content or density common ones are Brix, Oechsle and SG (specific gravity). We use Oechsle but SG is probably the most used density scale worldwide so we will be translating our formulas to SG for you to use at home The Oechsle scale is based on the weight of a liquid, minus the weight of the water in the liquid. The specific weight 1 litre (1¾ pints)of water is 1,000 g (2 lb 4 oz) which is 0 on the Oechsle scale. If 1 litre (1¾ pints) of liquid weighs 1,080 g (2lb 7oz), it means it's 80 degrees Oechsle. To convert this in to SG is really simple: 80 Oechsle is 1.080 SG and 1.080 SG is 80 Oechsle, more or less. There is a slight differential that changes exponentially but there is no real need to be that picky: this simple translation will do fine for these types of fermentations.

To measure the sugar content using a hydrometer, carefully place the hydrometer in a test tube or hydrometer jar and add a little of the freshly pressed juice, so that the hydrometer starts to float. Once it has stabilized and moves neither up nor down you can take the SG reading.

Our formula

We tend to use the following simplified formula:

Potential alcohol content = (Oechsle degrees x 2.55) / 19

The reason you multiply your Oechsle degrees by 2.55 is because each Oechsle degree is equivalent to approximately 2.55 g (¹⁄₁₆ oz) of sugar per litre (1¾ pints). If you then divide this sugar content by 19, which is an approximate value for how many grams of sugar is needed to convert into 1% alcohol, you will get the approximate potential alcohol content. If you think this seems like difficult maths, or if you simply prefer more exact values, there are many helpful tools on the internet where you simply fill in the Oechsle degrees or other unit for sugar content to get values for potential alcohol content and so on. Our apple juice is between 1.045 and 1.060 SG, which means it has around 115–155 g (4–5½ oz) of fermentable sugar per litre (1¾ pints) and a potential alcohol content of 6–8%. It can of course go below 1.045 and above 1.060, but if the fruit has the right ripeness, it is usually within this range.

Pears and sugar content

Pears are approximately in the same range as apples, but since not all the sugars in pears will ferment, and since these also contain carbohydrates that will read as sugar on the hydrometer, it might only be 1.035–1.050 SG from the 1.045–1.060 that the hydrometer shows that will ferment. This means that the sugar content is still 115–155 g (4–5½ oz) but the potential alcohol content is only 4.5–6.5% since only 90–130g (3¼–4½ oz) of the sugar is fermentable.

The same goes for plums, quince and some berries, but this can't be said for certain since all fruit is different and yearly variations will also have to be taken into account. To check this, we usually take a part of the fermenting juice and leave it in a warm place to finish off the fermentation as quickly as possible. Then we will know how much of the sugar in this particular juice will ferment. This is very useful information to make a note of, in order to know when to bottle or as an aid when blending fully fermented or almost fully fermented batches with others, especially if they are made with different types of fruit.

CIDER REVOLUTION!

48

FERME

Once you've got your lovely freshly pressed juice it's time to ferment it – a very exciting stage in the birth of a cider. It's also during the fermentation that you can really influence how your finished drink will turn out.

NTING

Our attitude to food and drink in general, and also to farming and cultivation, is that we want it to be natural. So, it goes without saying that we make our drinks without any additives. To create interesting drinks, especially those with a fairly low alcohol content, how you ferment the juice is very important.

Fermenting mainly means letting yeast cells convert the sugar in the juice to alcohol. In our view, the fruit's natural yeast cells are the best suited for this activity. They can convert the fruit's sugar into a more balanced drink, but above all, a drink with a broader flavour spectrum than if you added a commercial yeast strain. It makes the choice easy for us. Since we want to preserve the flavours of specific apple varieties, we want to use that particular apple's natural yeast – without any influences from other types of yeast. If you add yeast, you will steer the drink in a specific direction and will make it more one-dimensional and uniform, removing the fruit's individual aromas, flavour and sense of place. A natural fermentation is complex: many different yeast strains, bacteria and other organisms can influence the early stage, but eventually the strongest yeast strain will take over and finish off the fermentation. The result will be a much more interesting drink.

Of course, you can choose whether you want to add commercial yeast. It usually means that the fermentation will start sooner, and you will minimize the risk of unwelcome bacterial growth or stuck fermentation. But it's called 'turbo yeast' for a reason, so if you're aiming for a slower fermentation it might not be the best choice. We don't use commercial yeast ourselves since we think it kills the soul and energy of cidermaking.

Slow fermentation

We advocate slow fermentation in order to extract more flavour and aromas from the fruit. This means that we ferment at lower temperatures (6–10°C/43–50°F), so that the sugar content in the juice is reduced slowly. To be on the safe side and to get the fermentation going quickly, before unwelcome bacteria have a chance to take over, we start off the fermentation at slightly higher temperatures (16–20°C/61–68°F), before transferring the vats to a colder place just after the fermentation has started. That way we calm down the yeast and the fermentation speed. The premises we use for fermentation aren't temperature controlled, but we try to move the fermentation vessels around between rooms at different temperatures to control it as much as we can. Of course, each year will be different because of fluctuating outdoor temperatures. Trying to control the temperature can sometimes prolong the fermentation for several weeks or even months. The longer the fermentation goes on, the more effect it will have on the balance and expression of the juice. A nice, balanced juice can become thin and bland after fermentation, while a relatively neutral juice can become fantastic after fermentation. So we taste all the vats during the fermentation to ensure that they're going in the right direction, but also to get a feel for which varieties might be suited for blending later and which will do just fine on their own.

Sulphur?

If you want to stabilize the juice you can add sulphur in various forms. However, this will affect all the bacteria in the fermentation and will also kill off some or all yeast strains that appear naturally on the fruit. You might also need to add commercial yeast to be able to start and keep the fermentation going until the sugar has fully fermented, and you will probably end up having to add more sulphur as you go along. This can create an increasingly sterile product, where the flavours will be masked by a layer of additives. We don't use sulphur, but if you think it feels safer, perhaps try a couple of batches with commercial yeast and sulphur to give you enough experience to eventually become brave enough to leave out the additives.

The fermentation starts

Regardless of which method you choose, the fermentation will hopefully start. The juice, which is usually brown and cloudy when freshly pressed, and not that lovely juice colour that you might initially have imagined, will start to bubble and smell slightly acidic. The first sign of fermentation before you start to see or hear the fizzing, is a pungent salty smell that is very sharp. This is the carbon dioxide that is formed during the fermentation. If you can smell it, the fermentation has got going. Once the fermentation has started and carbon dioxide is formed, the risk of unwanted bacterial growth is also minimized. The fermentation will create a protective atmosphere in the fermentation vessel, which prevents unwelcome bacteria from getting to the fermenting liquid. This means that it's possible to ferment in open vats if you would like to have more oxygen flow during the fermentation. Open vats can, however, cause oxidation and may result in a spoiled cider, so it's not something we recommend for beginners.

Fermenting together or separately

We sometimes ferment different apple and pear varieties in separate fermentation vats and then blend them together later in the process. There are pros and cons with this approach. Juices in separate fermentation vats can ferment quicker or at a higher pH value than if they had fermented together, and there is a risk of imbalances developing during the fermentation. So if we have small volumes from many different varieties, we always ferment them together. The smaller the volume, the bigger the risk of complications, bacteria, stuck fermentation and so on. From our experience of making smaller batches, using smaller vats, the fermentation will become more unstable and the result is usually inferior. This is why it's better to blend smaller amounts of juice together to get a decent volume. If you want to make batches that are less than 10 litres (2.2 gallons), it's important that the vat is always filled to the brim, with no air pockets at the top.

Using pears

If you use pears, a part of the sugar content that you have measured won't ferment; the same goes for plums and many berries. It can therefore be a good idea to keep track of how much pear you mix in and to set a small amount of pure pear juice aside to ferment quickly, next to a radiator for example. Once it has finished fermenting, you can measure the sugar content to calculate how much of the sugar won't ferment in your large batch. Here's an example of how to calculate with pears:
10 litres (2.2 gallons) cider has fermented to 1.020 SG.
2 litres (3½ pints) of the cider are made from pears (that is, 20% of the cider is pear). When your test fermentation of pure pear juice is finished it stops at 1.010 SG. The formula will then be: 1.010SG = 10SG*0.2 (*% of the cider that is pear*) = 2SG =1.002SG that won't ferment. Which leaves you with 1.018 'fermentable' SG in your cider.

Racking

We're after a slow fermentation since, in our experience, this creates more aromatic notes and complexity and makes the cider better suited for ageing. Once the juice has started to ferment, we therefore want to remove some of the 'dead' yeast (lees) in order to slow down the fermentation. By transferring the cider into another fermentation vessel, we remove the lees from the bottom of the vat and are thus left with less active yeast. Different apples, pears and other fruits vary greatly, so learning when it's time to rack takes a bit of experience and an appetite for experimenting.

If you're unsure, you'll have to check the sugar content often. When it's decreasing rapidly, you can go ahead and rack. This is something that will vary from year to year, depending on how much sunlight the fruit has been exposed to, the temperatures during the year and so on. Some years you might even have to rack several times because the yeast is so active that it develops lees over a longer period of time. Picking fruit at an earlier stage of ripening could reduce the intensity of the yeast, and you might have to wait for longer, or not rack at all, to make sure you've got enough yeast to last through the whole fermentation process.

Depending on how slow a fermentation you would like, and how clean you want the cider to be, both in terms of appearance and flavour, you can rack as many times as you want to get rid of the 'dead' yeast. If you add more new juice it can come to life and start fermenting again. We usually say that cider that needs racking is 'dirty' and the result you get is therefore 'clean'.

56

Fermentation vats

As a cidermaker you have a great deal of choice when it comes to fermentation vessels. The material you use for fermenting and ageing will give the drink different characteristics. If you choose a neutral material such as plastic, fibreglass or steel, you won't get any flavour from the material but instead a fruitier and 'simpler' profile without too much oxidation.

Plastic is the cheapest and the most flexible, while glass and steel are more rigid materials that make the drink more restrained and reductive. Fibreglass is somewhere in the middle. If you instead choose a material that breathes, such as wood, concrete or clay, you will get both flavour and structure from the material. The drink can be influenced in various ways depending on the type of wood the barrel is made out of, or the type and thickness of the clay.

In addition to releasing flavours, vessels made from wood and clay will create the right conditions for micro-oxygenation. This will result in a more stable product since the cider is exposed to a very small amount of oxygen over a long period of time. Micro-oxygenation creates a kind of immunity against oxygen. If the liquid hasn't had any contact with oxygen during fermentation it will become used to being without it and can get a shock when it eventually comes into contact with it.

Regardless of which fermentation vats you use, it's good to fill them up to avoid getting too much air inside the vats. Unless oxidation is something you're aiming for.

Size and shape

The fermentation will become more stable and the risk of oxidation smaller if you use larger vats. Oxidation can mean a duller end result with over-ripe notes of fruit or a vinegary taste which is not very nice – unless it's a characteristic you are aiming to achieve.

The less contact with air and the vat the juice has the better. It is especially important to minimize the surface at the top of the fermentation vat in order to retain fruitiness and freshness in the drink. The shape and the size of the vat are therefore important since the contact the cider has with the internal surface of the vat will vary depending on the size of the vat. The size of the vat can also speed up or slow down the fermentation – the area of contact between the liquid and the yeast that settles at the bottom will have a certain amount of influence.

Depending on what type of press you use, and also what fruit you're pressing, you can expect a 50–80% yield. Meaning that 1 kg (2 lb 4 oz) of fruit will give 500–800 ml (18–28 fl oz) of juice (and sometimes even more). At the fermentation stage, the juice will expand slightly since it contains a lot of sediment that will increase in size when it starts to ferment and form carbon dioxide – choose the size of your vat accordingly.

If you choose to ferment the juice together with leftovers from the pressing (read more about post-maceration below) it's good to use open fermentation vats so that you can push down the fruit cap that forms during the fermentation and take it out again easily when it's time for the second pressing.

Start simple

There is also an financial aspect to the choice of vats. Plastic containers and vats are simple and cheap, oak barrels and handmade clay amphorae are expensive. If you are trying cidermaking for the first time, a couple of plastic containers will be enough; you can buy 30-litre (62/3-gallon) plastic buckets with removable lids from most home brewing shops. Take the opportunity to buy an airlock too, which will release the carbon dioxide without letting in any oxygen.

Our own choice of vats has been simple since we like a pared-back style where the fruit is allowed to speak for itself. Besides, we haven't been able to afford to buy many wooden barrels. In the future, however, we would consider fermenting different types of cider in different vessels to enhance certain aromas and flavours and to make the cider more suitable for ageing. We actually used a 250-litre (55-gallon) clay jug, a so-called amphora, in our first year to ferment apple juice from an old Bramley tree. The result from this ancient winemaking method turned out fantastically, if we do say so ourselves.

Post-maceration

While we're on the theme of fermenting, we'd like to introduce various post-maceration methods that we use – which you can read more about on page 127. By using the leftovers from the pressing and adding some of them to the fermentation vat, you can extract even more character from the skin and core.

To prevent the press leftovers oxidizing too much, we add them to the juice directly after pressing, but there aren't really any rules that say this is right or wrong. You are looking for some degree of oxidation in any case, so there aren't any exact timings. Waiting longer to add the press leftovers to the juice could, however, mean an increased risk of unwanted bacterial growth.

The exact ratio between press leftovers and juice is difficult to pinpoint, but since you will need to stir the mixture relatively often it's good to avoid making it too compact and heavy, in order to make it easier to work with. It's worth noting that the press leftovers will soak up the juice like a sponge, so if you add 20–25% press leftovers to the juice it will still feel like most of the vat is filled with press leftovers.

The cap

To prevent the growth of mould or other bacteria on the surface it's important to push down the cap that forms at the top as a result of the carbon dioxide production. This cap will give the cider a more oxidized or mature note since it is stirred back into the cider on a daily basis. Maceration leads to a higher oxidation and more tannin structure, which early on in the cider's life will give a very rustic and over-extracted flavour, and you lose some of the fruit. With time, however, this rustic feel gets more rounded and you will get a good balance and structure instead – which gives the cider more energy and makes it more suitable for ageing. Meaning that with a little patience and short periods of stirring, you can make completely different styles of cider using the same apple or pear variety.

More flavour

We also use post-maceration to more directly 'flavour' our cider with other types of fruit and berries. The maceration time depends on the type of berries or fruit we use, and we usually do this fairly late in the fermentation process. Once the cider is well on the way to becoming fully fermented, we add ripe whole berries that are left to macerate for the final week or weeks, to add flavour and also give structure to the cider. These berries or fruits are usually too low in sugar or too aromatic to use on their own, but in blends or as an added flavouring they are fantastic. It feels great to pick something in the garden or from the hedgerow and use it to give the cider a completely different character. These flavour additions also help to balance the drink and make it more interesting if the base if too neutral or if you just think it lacks something exciting.

Since we only use natural products and aren't big advocates of chaptalization (the process of adding sugar mainly to increase the alcohol content) we have sometimes made cider with honey instead. This might sound like double standards, but since honey is very aromatic and sweet it will give a dimension that you can't achieve from fruit alone. To call this version a cider is a matter of opinion, but it's good to know that, with only a small amount of honey, you can create an interesting drink where the main aim isn't to increase the alcohol content but to create more aromatic notes and structure. The taste can vary greatly depending on where the honey comes from, or what time of the year it was made.

Blending

Once it's time for bottling, there are a number of choices to consider. Tasting the cider regularly during the fermentation is good to get a feel for the fruit and the drink you are working with. If you have several fermentations on the go with different kinds of fruit, you have a golden opportunity to create the optimal cider. The idea behind blending is to create a balance between acidity, sweetness, bitterness and sometimes minerality. You can also create a longer finish and more mouth feel as well as emphasizing various characteristics from the different varieties. By blending together juice from different apple varieties that have been harvested in the same place, you can try to find an expression that represents both the shared terroir and each apple variety's character.

Sugar content

For blending, we use large vats that are similar to the ones we use for fermenting. First, we measure the sugar content in each separate vat to make sure the blend will be successful. Since all apple varieties will ferment at different speeds and since they will usually have started fermenting at different times, it can be the case that some are fully fermented and matured while others still have a lot of sugar content left. You can bottle at different sugar levels depending on whether you want to remove the lees after bottle fermenting, using the disgorging method (see page 85), or whether you want to keep the lees in the bottle. When disgorging, you open the cap you put in place when bottling, and therefore lose the pressure that has built up in the bottle. In that case it's better to bottle earlier, with more sugar, than if you want to keep the sediment and get a slightly more fruity and cloudy cider. Regardless of the method you choose, a sugar content of 10–30 g (¼–1 oz) per litre (1¾ pints) is a good level to ensure the bottle fermentation is safe, without any exploding bottles.

Pearling bubbles

We prefer bottling later with less sugar to get a lightly pearling cider, rather than a lot of bubbles that will dull down the expression from the fruit. It's also worth mentioning that cider doesn't have to have any bubbles at all. Some cider is still and is bottled once fully fermented. This will often make the cider more complex and vinous, which can be very interesting. Since the alcohol content is fairly low, there is, however, a greater chance that the cider will spoil or become infested with unwanted bacteria. This is because carbon dioxide is produced throughout the fermentation process; it creates a protective environment in the fermentation vat and later in the bottle. When fermentation has finished, bacteria have a much greater chance of success fully attacking the cider.

Bottling

After any blending it is time to transfer the cider to bottles or other closed containers. Bottling is probably the most satisfying, but also the most anxiety-inducing, stage in the whole process, since you can no longer control the end result to the same extent. Although, in the unlikely event that you are not happy with a cider that has been bottled, you can open the bottles and pour the contents into a vat, age it and then add new juice to it the following year or even later. We bottle at 1.003 to 1.004 SG, or 1.007 to 1.010 SG when we want to disgorge.

Bottling can be done in a number of different ways – the important thing is to transfer the beverage to the bottle without too much sediment and lees. The simplest method uses

gravity. If the fermentation vat has a tap on the side, you can use this for bottling; if not, you can siphon the liquid (see page 83).

When we bottle, we lift up the vat and attach a manual bottle-filling machine that uses vacuum. It's a simple bottle-filling method that is relatively cheap and that doesn't affect the cider by introducing too much air. The disadvantage is that it takes time to fill a lot of bottles, since it's dependent on how quickly the liquid flows through the pipes. Using a pump is a quicker process, but also involves more exposure to air – which can be good for some cider but can mean unwelcome oxidation.

If you choose to bottle without disgorging later on, take care to bottle cleanly. That means racking the cider the day before so that hardly any sediment remains. When you bottle, make sure the cider is 'alive', meaning that it's still fermenting. Put your ear up close and listen – is there any activity going on or is it as quiet as a library? Sometimes the fermentation after you've racked the cider to get rid of the gross lees. If the fermentation is stuck, you should shake the vat gently and leave it at room temperature for a day or so. If that doesn't help, you'll have to add a little bit of freshly squeezed juice and leave the vat at room temperature until you notice fermentation activity again.

Bottles and capping

Classic 330 ml (11 2/3 fl oz) bottles will mean that bottling takes longer, and there are more caps to put on, but they are very convenient when you're having a picnic in the park. If you are disgorging, 750 ml (25 fl oz) bottles are good. You can reuse empty glass bottles as long as you clean them thoroughly.

After the bottle has been filled, it's important to close it quickly to prevent oxidation and any bacteria getting into the bottle neck. The fact that the cider is still fermenting, creates a protective environment in itself, but it's still good to close it as soon as possible.

Bottles with a swing top mean it's easy to release the pressure and then quickly close them again, if necessary. The simplest and cheapest way to close bottles is to use caps and a hand-operated bottle capper.

Once the bottling is done, it's mostly time and patience that are required from the cidermaker. Now comes the most boring but most important stage, ageing. Once you have bottled your drink, it's more or less a matter of waiting, and maybe eventually trying the technique known as disgorging.

AGEING
AND BOTTLE

FERMENTATION

The cider now needs time to mature and bottle ferment, which will create the fizz. You may have to wait for anything from a few months up to a few years before the cider has finished fermenting, has stabilized and is ready to drink.

Ageing can be done in various ways, but our favourite method is to lay all the bottles on their sides, in a container that you can shake. Try to shake them at least once the first week. Shaking the bottles is a way to encourage the fermentation in case it has stalled at the bottling stage. Usually there aren't any problems, but it's good as a little insurance for peace of mind. Turn a bottle upside down and – unless you use a bottle made of dark glass – you can almost see if it has fermented and created a few bubbles or not.

The more complex fruit you use, the more time in the bottle is needed before the end is in sight. And since we've only been producing for a couple of years, we don't have a direct answer to how long you should wait or exactly how long the various beverages will keep for. The only thing we do know is that most bottles have been opened too early. Trying the cider as it ages is interesting of course and it might be good for checking the carbon dioxide levels, but early on you won't be able to detect many of the flavours that you did during the fermentation. If you are content with a slightly cloudy and fruity cider, you don't have to disgorge, which would otherwise be the next step.

Disgorging

To get a clearer cider, you can remove the lees that have built up during the bottle fermentation, using a technique called disgorging. In champagne production this is done after the second fermentation, but in the case of pét-nat, which is the most similar to our method, you can do it after the first fermentation (read more about this on page 125).

There are several benefits of disgorging – not just that the drink will look 'cleaner' and nicer. The flavour profile will become crisper and the drink will feel cleaner in both aroma and flavour. Since the bottle is opened once after the fermentation has finished, the drink will be 'finished' sooner. Sometimes it can take a bit longer for non-disgorged cider and wine to come into its own. But to age longer with the lees, or to keep the lees altogether, will also retain the youthfulness of the drink for longer. The bubbles will calm down a lot if you remove the lees, however, so you don't have to worry about unexpected volcanoes and unwanted imitations of the Grand Prix winners' podium.

If you want to disgorge, you will need to place all the bottles upside down in a cool place for a couple of days. Give them a shake as you turn them over. This will make the lees settle down into the bottle neck. Then you remove the cap while holding the bottle upside down: the yeast will shoot out and you'll get a cleaner cider. We recommend you do this outside; you can see how it's done on page 85. If you choose to disgorge, it's not as important to bottle cleanly, by carefully racking the cider before bottling it. But the dirtier you bottle, the wilder the bubbles will become, and you will lose more cider when disgorging. Since the sugar content is higher when bottling for disgorging, the yeast can also be stronger, which means that you usually won't have a problem with stuck fermentation.

It's best to wait a couple of months before disgorging: the longer you wait, the 'creamier' the cider will become since it sits on the lees for longer. Next time you drink champagne, check the bottle and you may see the disgorgement date. It's just a bit of boasting to show off how long the bubbly has been sitting on the lees.

Skipping disgorging?

You can miss out on a great deal of depth and complexity in your cider if you choose to disgorge it. If you bottle it cleanly enough it's mostly just the lees from the bottle fermentation that remains. If the bottle has stood upright for some time, and you pour the cider carefully, the lees will stay in place at the bottom until the last glass. The yeast will give the cider a creamier and more balanced flavour profile. We use disgorging for some of our cider varieties but leave many of them un-disgorged, to let the yeast play a bigger role in the flavour. If the bubbles continue to behave, the cider can develop in very exciting ways – even though it may take longer for it to reach its peak.

Defects and troubleshooting

Making cider can be a walk in the park without any complications whatsoever. This has been the case for us in most instances. But despite garden fruit being quite forgiving to work with, unexpected things can happen, especially when you are making drinks without any additives. One early problem that can arise is that the juice doesn't start to ferment. The longer the juice is left to stand without fermenting, the greater the chance of unwanted bacterial growth, oxidation and so on. The way to save it can be to place the fermentation vessel in a warm place and possibly shake it to activate the yeast that sits at the bottom. Don't despair if this doesn't work on the first attempt. Leave the vat in a warm room and shake it a few more times over the next few days. If this doesn't help, you can try adding freshly pressed juice that contributes new yeast. Once the fermentation kicks in, you can put the vat back in a cooler place.

Defects or off aromas are usually created by microorganisms that live their own little lives in the cider, but as long as you keep an eye on the fermentation you can prevent or counteract them in most cases. Some 'defects' can be difficult to define and split the cider world into different camps. Something that is completely undrinkable to some can be perceived by others as making the cider more interesting. These discussions aren't unusual since naturally produced drinks are more alive and will change more over time in comparison with conventionally produced beverages.

Unless you taste your apples and juice continuously, from harvest via juicing, fermentation, blending, all the way to bottling, you will find it difficult to know what has or hasn't happened. Therefore, our tip is to try it often, and preferably together with others so that you can discuss. Always start by taking some time for yourself and your journal. Then you will have formed your own opinion before the discussions get a bit wild.

If you suspected early on that things started to happen that could develop into some kind of defect, step one after bottling is to check the status. Sometimes a drink may simply be going through a closed or bad phase that it will later come out of. In that case it's not a defect but only a phase in the development of the cider. As long as you can recognize elements in the drink from previous tastings, and as long as there aren't any drastic changes, you can remain relatively calm.

If you think the cider is continuing to go in the wrong direction and it has got worse since the last tasting, the defect is most likely a reality, unfortunately. People do have different levels of tolerance to smells, however, and are therefore more or less sensitive to defects.

How tannins, structures and acids will develop is difficult to predict, since they change over time. A cider with too many tannins or too high acidity will become more integrated, so that these aspects will be perceived as less intense after more time in the bottle. So, our tip is to bottle with higher levels of the character that you had in mind for the finished product, since everything will become less intense than it was during the fermentation process. Mastering this is largely a matter of experience.

Has your cider turned into vinegar?

One common phenomenon is that you might think that the fully fermented drink has turned to vinegar. You notice the heavily pungent smell that arises when acetic acid bacteria (acetobacter) take over and convert alcohol molecules into acetic acids. This can absolutely be the case, but often a low level of these acids can create an exciting and refreshing character, so this doesn't have to be a negative thing. In wine it is often referred to as volatile acidity and is something that some winemakers regard as their greatest enemy, while others aim for a light volatile balance in their wines to make them a bit fresher and more interesting.

To avoid acetic acid bacteria taking over in the finished drink, it's important that it doesn't come into contact with too much oxygen; this is particularly important if you ferment smaller volumes. The simplest way to avoid acetic acids is to add sulphur, but as long as you are careful with cleanliness and make sure you keep the fermentation vats approximately 90% full, you should also succeed with smaller batches. We also believe that an early micro-oxygenation (airing/racking) makes the cider stronger and more resistant to attacks from acetic acid.

If the acetic acids have taken hold, there is no way back and they will continue to grow until your cider has completely turned into vinegar. In the early stages you can save it by mixing it with new juice, or another fermented cider which doesn't have such volatile properties, and in this way neutralize the effect of these bacteria. They will remain in the beverage, but they won't grow fast enough to make vinegar, and with their slightly aggressive acidity, they can actually bring a welcome energy boost to a fairly one-dimensional cider.

Oxidation and other defects

Oxygen can also lead to oxidation of a fully fermented cider. The drink will become darker over time, and instead of notes of fresh fruit, it will be leathery and flat.

One debated 'defect' is a so-called yeast film, an often thin, slightly oily, fuzzy, dull film on the surface of the fully or almost fully fermented drink. It is formed when the yeast and the liquid react with oxygen, and if you haven't added any sulphur the liquid will create its own protection against oxidation. There are various types of wild yeast that can create this film. In the world of beer, and sometimes wine, they talk about Brettanomyces. The drink is then perceived as slightly dirty or tasting of cellar, and film yeast has therefore got a bad reputation, at least in the wine world. In the wine world they also talk about flor, which is common in certain wine styles and can be regarded as a cleaner type of yeast film. Flor will add saltiness and length to the drink (read more about flor on page 128). This type of development of the beverage can be regarded as both positive and negative – but everyone agrees that it provides character.

Another widely discussed defect is a mousy smell, or mousiness. Many people hate both the smell and the odd aftertaste, while others think the rodenty smell adds something to the drink. No one seems to know exactly what it is, or how it actually occurs. What is known, is that it relates to lactic acids in combination with certain yeast strains together with oxygen. Some say it's linked to the cultivation and how healthy the ground is where the plants or trees grow. There are as many theories as there are experts who discuss them.

Ropiness and oiliness are also terms where opinions are divided. These also relate to lactic acids in drinks that are high in acid, which in this case produce a gel-like liquid. When you pour it, the drink is viscous and resembles egg white. The flavour is unaffected, however, and you can simply break up the gel by a vigorous decanting or shaking. With ageing, it may dissolve completely by itself, so there is no reason to worry too much.

There are of course a range of other 'defects', so if you are worried you can always search online to try and figure out what the problem can be. The most important thing is to taste and make your own judgement as to whether the drink is okay or not.

BY

STEP

STEP-
-

Here we take you through the stages and techniques of cidermaking. The size of the equipment may vary, it's possible to make cider in everything from a PET bottle to gigantic tanks, but the steps are the same. The equipment shown in the photos is suitable for those who want to make batches of approximately 25 litres (5½ gallons) of finished cider at a time.

STEP-BY-STEP

1. Sort the fruit, discard any bad specimens.

80

2. Wash the fruit in cold water.

3. Crush in a fruit crusher. This model is hand-turned.

4. If you want to make a **pre-maceration**, you just leave the crushed fruit to stand and turn brown.

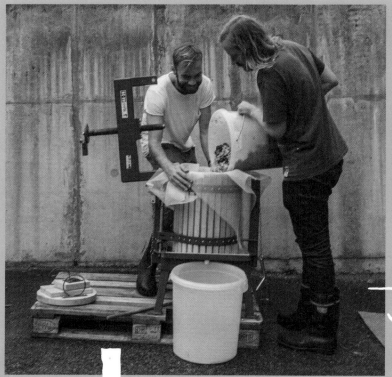

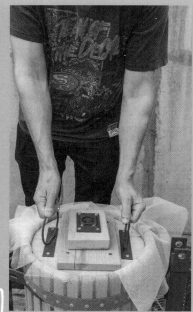

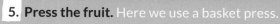

5. Press the fruit. Here we use a basket press.

6. Taste the juice and measure the sugar content using a hydrometer.

7. Leave the juice to ferment with an airlock in a dark place, preferably at a temperature around 8–10°C (46–50°F). If you want to get the fermentation started quickly, you can leave the vat at 20°C (68°F) until it gets going. The lees will settle at the bottom.

8. If you want to make a **post-maceration** you add crushed fruit, whole berries or other flavourings to the fermenting juice.

9. Rack the cider by siphoning it over into another vat. Create a flow by sucking at the end of the hose that hangs out of the vat. Make sure that the end submerged in the fermentation vat sits above the lees, so that the sediment doesn't get transferred over. Repeat before bottling if you want a clearer cider.

10. Bottle your beverage using a siphon. Cut off the flow once the bottle is full and swap for a new empty bottle before releasing the clamp again. As long as there is liquid in the vessel and the level is higher up than the bottle you are filling you can continue. Avoid the lees at the bottom of the vat.

11. Close the bottles using a bottle capper.

12. Age the bottles in a cool, dark place.

13. If you want to remove the lees, you will need to **disgorge**. Place the bottles upside down for a few days so that the lees gather in the neck. Open it while holding it downwards at an angle, and stop the flow with your thumb as soon as you have got rid of the lees. Be quick! If needed, top up with juice from another bottle and then cap it again.

14. After ageing, it's time for cider tasting.

Making cider in the kitchen

If you are curious about cidermaking, it's perfectly possible to experiment with small batches in your kitchen. Even without a garden or a garage you can, using kitchen equipment you already have at home and perhaps a few additions, start your cider career.

1. For juicing on a very small scale, one simple option is a centrifugal juicer. It will easily transform various fruits into juice. If you haven't got a centrifugal juicer, don't worry, and above all, don't buy one solely for this purpose. If you use a standard grater, the result will be even better and more similar to standard juicing than if you use a centrifugal juicer. With a grater, you will get a fruit pulp that you can pre-macerate and then press.

2. For fermentation vats, you can use thoroughly cleaned PET or glass bottles, or small plastic buckets. An airlock is useful to have but not essential. Screwing the caps on halfway will let air out, but not a lot will get in. It also keeps the flies away.

3. Pressing can be a bit more difficult in the kitchen, but one simple method is to use a colander with a press cloth. If you don't have a press cloth, a tea towel or an old bed sheet will do the trick. If you want a cruder juice with more sediment, you can try using a sieve. Place the grated pulp in a colander or sieve and press with your hands so that as much liquid as possible gets separated from the more solid parts of the pulp.

4. Fill the bottles with the juice, but only up to 75–80% of the bottle's volume. If you fill the containers all the way up, there is a chance they will bubble over when they start to ferment, with cleaning and lost juice as a result. It's a good idea to use a funnel or something else that makes the pouring easier, but don't forget to clean everything you use beforehand.

5. In most cases the fermentation will start fairly quickly, especially if the bottles are left at room temperature. Once the fermentation gets going, it's time to rack the juice into new bottles. You can do this using a food-grade hose that you insert as far down the bottle as you can without unsettling the sediment at the bottom. Then you siphon the contents into another bottle (see the step-by-step on page 83). If you use PET bottles or other bottles with an indent at the base, the sediment may be settled enough to make it possible to pour straight into the new bottle – however, once you've started pouring, you can't turn the bottle upright again and then continue pouring. If you do, the yeast will get stirred up and you will transfer the sediment over to the next bottle. At this stage, you can fill the bottles up a bit more, but it's always good to leave a bit of room during the fermentation. Now, transfer the bottles to a cooler place.

6. When the fermentation is underway, all you have to do is to sit back and let the yeast do its job on the sugar in the juice. However, it's a good idea to check it regularly to make sure nothing unexpected has happened. The fermentation can get stuck or the liquid flow over, for example. Take the opportunity to check the sugar content as well, to follow the fermentation curve. If you think the sugar is decreasing too quickly, you can do another round of racking to get rid of some of the yeast and slow down the fermentation.

7. Once you have reached the required sugar content (see recipes further on in the book), it's time for bottling. It's a good idea to rack the liquid a final time before filling up the final bottles. At this stage it can also be good to have a hose for siphoning.

For ageing, it's easiest to use bottles with a screw cap. You can also use clean beer bottles, but then you will have to buy some form of bottle capper and some caps. You will find simpler models for around a tenner in home brewing shops.

Thoroughly clean both the bottle and the cap using boiling water. As soon as you have filled it, close each bottle. Leave a few centimetres (an inch) when you fill the bottles. Now you just have to wait a couple of months until it's time for cider tasting and hopefully euphoric shouts of joy.

Here we have developed suggestions for ciders that you can make at home. It's impossible to give an exact template, since we are reliant on a natural process where the fruit's yeast strains and sugar content, temperature during the fermentation and many other parameters will come into play. Sometimes it's quick and sometimes it takes time. Some ciders we have made have taken four to five months, others just a week – but we will try to guide you with the experience we have gained along the way.

You will find the techniques and various practical steps in the step-by-step guide on pages 80–85. It's a good idea to be outside for some of the steps so that you don't have to clean floors and work surfaces.

RECIPE

DiSCO CiDER (dance-friendly)

A classic disco cider should be light and fresh and pack in a lot of energy. By this we mean that it should be alive and zesty. The flavour of the finished drink is fruity and dry and shouldn't be too complex. You should want to drink a couple of glasses without too much contemplation and the drink should be refreshing and thirst quenching so that the dancing can continue. If you don't like dancing, it's also great as an aperitif all year round – but it's best during the slightly warmer months. If you want to serve it to complement food, think along the lines of vegetable-based nibbles or a picnic in the summer sun?

The apple varieties matter less, but it's better to use slightly simpler and aromatic varieties since they have a high level of acid and the right amount of aromatic flavour, resulting in a dry but balanced cider with refreshing acidity. If it feels like the cider is lacking in energy, it's a good idea to mix in more juice during the fermentation in order to prolong it and to bottle it before the cider has fully fermented.

Suitable fruit

Ingrid Marie, Cox's Orange Pippin and Aroma are common garden varieties in many parts of Sweden and are suitable for this style. It's best to use fruit from young trees since it is extra fruity and youthful without too much complexity or minerality.

Aim to use fruit early on in its ripening process since the acidity will be highest then and the apples will make a nice clean juice. If the fruit is over-ripe it will turn into mush when crushing and pressing it. Using fruit at a later stage of ripening will give you an over-ripe, more tropical feel and a flavour that edges towards apple sauce – which you absolutely don't want in a dance-friendly cider.

A good start is to try and gather at least 50 kg (110 lb) of apples from these fresh varieties, which is approximately 3 paper carrier bags. With this you'll be able to make around 30 litres (62/3 gallons) of juice and later get around 25 litres (5½ gallons) of fermented cider.

Duration

For the volume mentioned above, you can expect to work for a few hours on the first day. Sorting and washing will take 1 hour. Crushing will take around the same time, and the pressing will take 2 hours.

When using simple apple varieties, the bottle ageing will often be quicker and if you are lucky with the fermentation both in the vat and the bottle, you can start sampling the bottles around 3 months after harvesting.

Preparation

Wash the fruit in cold water. Crush the fruit and leave it to pre-macerate for a short while, a maximum of 3–4 hours, by simply leaving it to stand. Since the fruit is fairly sensitive, the pulp will turn brown relatively quickly, which is a sign that it can be pressed quickly and will give a simple but energetic juice with strong fruit character.

Press the fruit pulp and collect the juice in a thoroughly cleaned plastic container that is slightly larger than the volume you intend to press, so that there is space for some expansion during the fermentation.

Now is the time to measure the sugar content and make a note of any other things you want to check before the fermentation starts. To avoid getting too much alcohol in the disco cider, it should be around 1.045–1.050 SG, which means the finished cider will have an alcohol content of around 6–6.5%.

Fermentation

If we assume that your fruit is fairly early on in its ripening, it may mean that the fermentation will take some time to start. It can therefore be a good idea to place the fermentation vat in a slightly warmer room, around 20°C (68°F), to get the fermentation going.

As soon as the fermentation starts, rack the cider into a new vat to remove most of the sediment and to calm down the speed of the fermentation. If you are unsure whether the fermentation has started or not, put an ear to the vat and listen out for the bubbles – if you can hear it fizzing, the fermentation has started. Now you can move the cider somewhere colder; a garage that stays around 8–10°C (46–

50°F) is good and means the fermentation should take around 1–1½ months.

Blending

This style of cider doesn't need blending with other juice, but if you think it lacks energy or aromatics you can add new juice. This will prolong the fermentation. Once you get to the right sugar content, you can bottle it to retain the energy.

If you want to blend different vats of similar disco cider, you can do so. It's best to do this when the sugar content is a bit higher than what you want to bottle it at, preferably 1.010 SG (approximately 27g/1 oz sugar per litre/1¾ pints) or more to allow the different parts to ferment together for a while.

Bottling, bottle fermenting and ageing

When the sugar content is at the right level, it's time to bottle – see below for examples of sugar content levels to bottle at:

If you are not disgorging:
approx. 1.003–1.005 SG

If you are disgorging:
approx. 1.008–1.010 SG

Since a lot of the energy sits in the lees, we recommend keeping them in the bottle and not disgorging the disco cider, but is up to you. Make sure to bottle as cleanly as possible if you don't disgorge, to prevent bottles turning into volcanoes. If the bubbles bounce against the lees and multiply, it will create an involuntary champagne (cider)-spraying situation that is difficult to get out of.

The answer to the question of how long the disco cider should age, is down to when you want to drink it – we think a suitable time is when the sun is shining and the temperature is warming up. So, try it during late spring or early summer, when the bottles have aged for a couple of months.

CHAT CIDER (the aperitif)

This is the cider style we probably make the most. It's not too complex or difficult to understand – just like a good chat with a friend. It should taste crisp but still have a mature expression. It's a great start to the evening and can also be a perfect palate cleanser during the meal.

In comparison with the disco cider (page 92), it's the apple varieties that make the difference rather than the process. If you're a bit sensitive to high acidity, which you often get with these fully dry cider styles, adding some pears is a natural way to balance the acidity with sweetness. But don't think you'll be able to create a super sweet cider like the big brand, shop-bought drinks just because you use a lot of pears. It will still be similar to a classic dry French cider.

Suitable fruit

To create a more complex cider it's important that you select the right fruit varieties and preferably also that the trees they have grown on have reached a certain age. We prefer slightly older apple varieties that aren't commonly cultivated any more but that can still be found in many gardens – if you are able to pick Filippa, Gravenstein or similar varieties with a tropical character and a lot of yellow/green fruitiness, they are perfect for creating a broader spectrum of flavours and aromas. It's best to pick the fruit at optimal ripeness, when the first fruits have started to fall off the trees. You can also complement with pears, if you find fresh, sprightly varieties that give a good balance to the acidity by adding a bit of sweetness.

If you have different apple varieties, you can ferment them together from the beginning. If you want to use pears in your chat cider, it is a good idea to ferment them separately, which means more of a pear flavour will come through when you blend it with the apple juice. In our experience, apples tend to take over if you ferment pears and apples together.

Try to collect at least 50 kg (110 lb) of apples, or alternatively 40 kg (88 lb) apples and 10 kg (22 lb) pears. We think around 20% pear gives a good balance. Then you'll be able to make around 30 litres (6⅔ gallons) of juice and eventually get 25 litres (5½ gallons) of fermented cider.

Duration

For the volume mentioned above, you can expect a few hours of working time on the first day. Sorting and washing will take 1 hour. Crushing will take around the same time, and the pressing will take 2 hours.

When using less aromatic apple varieties, the bottle ageing will often be quicker and if you are lucky with the fermentation both in the vat and the bottle, you can start sampling the bottles around 4–6 months after harvesting.

Preparation

Wash the fruit in cold water. Crush the fruit and leave it to pre-macerate for a short while, approximately 4–6 hours, by simply leaving it to stand. Since the fruit is fairly sensitive, the pulp will turn brown relatively quickly, which is a sign that it can be pressed quickly and will give a simple but energetic juice with strong fruit character.

If you are using pears of a less aromatic variety, for example Alexander Lucas, they can benefit from macerating for a little longer, possibly overnight. Alternatively, crush the pears first but press them last.

Press the fruit pulp and collect the juice into a thoroughly cleaned plastic container that is slightly larger than the volume you intend to press, so that there is space for some expansion during the fermentation. Now is the time to measure the sugar content and make a note of any other things you want to check before the fermentation starts. Note that if you are using pears, some of the sugar won't ferment; read more about this on page 46.

Fermentation

It can be a good idea to place the fermentation vat in a slightly warmer room, around 20°C (68°F), to get the fermentation going. As soon as the fermentation starts, rack the cider into a new vat to remove most of the sediment and to calm down the speed of the fermentation. If you are unsure whether the fermentation has started or not, put an ear to the vat and listen out for the bubbles – if you can hear it fizzing the fermentation has started. Now you can move the cider somewhere colder; a garage that stays around 8–10°C (46–50°F) is good and means the fermentation should take around 1–1½ months, but it could also take considerably longer.

Blending
If you want to blend different vats of similar chat cider you can do so. It's best to do this when the sugar content is a bit higher than what you want to bottle it at, preferably 1.010 SG (approximately 27g/1oz sugar per 1 litre/1¾ pints) or more to allow the different parts to ferment together for a while.

Bottling, bottle fermenting and ageing
When the sugar content is at the right level, it's time to bottle. Remember, if you are using pears, not all of the sugars will ferment. For us, it's usually around 20% but it varies from year to year and pear to pear.

If you are not disgorging:
approx. 1.003–1.005 SG

If you are disgorging:
approx. 1.008–1.010 SG

The chat cider will benefit from disgorging to make it as crisp and fresh as possible. If you don't disgorge, make sure to bottle as cleanly as possible to prevent bottles turning into erupting volcanoes. The chat cider doesn't need to be aged for a particularly long time: a few months are enough.

ORANGE CIDER

Orange wine is something we are seeing more of in bars and restaurants. Just as the name suggests, the colour is usually orange or amber. The wine itself is fairly similar to red wine in structure but with flavours that are more associated with white wines made from dried grapes. The typical modern white wine is not usually macerated with the grape skins, meaning the colour is almost transparent. If the winemaker chooses to keep the grape skins in contact with the juice, the wine will become more or less orange, depending on how strong the white grapes' skins are.

The style and the method of making orange wine are actually very traditional; it has been made since time immemorial. Nowadays it's mostly associated with Georgia, Slovenia and south-eastern Europe.

During our first experiments using this method we noticed that the cider took a very long time to reach its full potential, but it becomes very complex, has some tannin structure and is more suitable for ageing than most.

Suitable fruit

Cox or other robust apples such as Gloster and Belle de Boskoop work well for skin contact. Around 50 kg (110 lb) of apples is a good amount to start with.

Duration

Allow an afternoon or a few hours for sorting, crushing and washing. This style also requires a lot of supervision and work during the first weeks, since you will need to push down the fruit cap that forms and then re-press the cap, leaving no more than a few days in between.

For the cider to become completely ready to drink, it will need ageing for at least 1 year, preferably longer. The more self-discipline, the better the result.

Preparation

Sort and wash the fruit in cold water. Crush the fruit and leave it to pre-macerate. We usually go for 24 hours of maceration before pressing, but do experiment leaving it for longer if you want to achieve a more mature style or for less time if you want a fresher cider.

Press the juice and add the skin leftovers to the fermentation vat. Use a generously-sized vat since the press leftovers will swell once fermentation starts. For 50 kg (110 lb) of apples, a 30-litre (6⅔-gallon) plastic fermentation vat (that can be bought from most homebrewing stores) will do the job well, and it comes with a lid that you can cover it with once you've stirred the juice. A good ratio to aim for is 20–25% skin leftovers in relation to juice, but feel free to experiment.

When the juice has started to ferment, which it will do quite quickly since there is a lot of wild yeast on the skin, a cap of press leftovers will form at the top. You will have to push this down regularly to prevent it from drying out and starting to grow mould. We usually use a plastic spade. The more frequently you push down the cap, the more contact the juice will get with the skin, and the more tannins and flavour it will get.

Fermentation

Try to measure the sugar content very frequently to keep an eye on the fermentation. It won't be the easiest thing to do due to the cap a fine conical strainer can be a useful tool. Remove the skins from the juice before it has finished fermenting. If you don't, everything will mix again, and it will become a lot more difficult to press the skins a second time – plus the cider is a lot more sensitive to oxidation and infections when it is not fermenting.

Then decide how hard to press the fruit cap. The second pressing will give even more tannins and structure, and we have never found that this has ever become overpowering.

You also need to take into consideration that the fermentation can be very quick since there is a lot of power in the yeast from the skins. After the second pressing we therefore recommend placing the vat somewhere cool and letting it settle and form a sediment; there will often be some residue at both the bottom and the top of the vat. You can rack it into a new vat fairly soon.

Blending
If the fermentation is too quick, a good solution could be to blend in a small amount of juice with higher sugar content before bottling. Of course, this will make your orange cider less orange. Try to blend so that the juices can ferment together for 1–3 SG.

Bottling, bottle fermenting and ageing
This is definitely a style that we think benefits from not being disgorged: you will get a more powerful and full-bodied cider and it will become even more suitable for ageing with a bit of lees left in the bottle. As always, take care to bottle as cleanly as possible if you are not disgorging – this can be difficult with orange cider since the colour is so intense that it can be a bit tricky to see how cloudy it actually is. Place the vat somewhere cool the week before bottling so that the liquid sediments well.

You can disgorge it too, of course, which will give a cleaner cider with clearer apple notes and it will be ready for consumption sooner. As we have already pointed out, this cider is a very good candidate for long ageing. Good sugar content for bottling is:

If you are not disgorging:
approx. 1.003–1.005 SG

If you are disgorging:
1.008–1.010 SG

BERNADOTTE CIDER (Swedish/French)

For many, the archetype of cider is French, and we often get asked how to make this particular style. The simple and probably only correct answer is that this style is best made in France, from cider apples picked in regions such as Brittany or Normandy where they have good local varieties and fruit trees as well as old traditions. However, since we want to help as much as possible, we can share a recipe that could possibly resemble a style that is a bit more French.

One way to achieve that coarse tannin-rich bitterness that you get from cider apples is to look for crab apples. We have talked very little about crab apples, mainly because we haven't worked with them much, but also because they vary an incredible amount from tree to tree and behave very differently from each other, which it makes it difficult to do crab apples justice in a book.

We know some real cider enthusiasts in Sweden who work almost exclusively with crab apples and have achieved outstanding results – always in small quantities, but just the right amount for home consumption. So, to try to make a cider in a French style, we recommend adding a small quantity of crab apples. Look along the edges of ditches or hedgerows and old forest roads and you will usually find the trees. Taste the fruit, think about it and try to find your favourite tree. The worse the crab apples taste, and the more you want to immediately spit them out, the better, in most cases.

Suitable fruit

Hardy and robust apples, preferably from very old trees and ideally as ripe as possible. Don't worry if they have 'caramelized' – as long as they aren't mouldy outside or inside, they are perfect. Use gloves, since over-ripe apples can be quite sticky. The level of ripeness also means a bit more work in the sorting process.

Varieties such as Bramley, Belle de Boskoop, Cox and Gloster are perfect and, as mentioned, if you can find a good crab apple tree, you have the opportunity to make a cider with the complex, slightly bitter, oxidative, over-ripe and acidic notes that are typical of French cider. Just 10% of crab apples will make an enormous difference. We also like this style made without crab apples and think it creates the maximum complexity from Scandinavian garden fruit.

Duration
Allow for a couple of hours of preparation time, plus a bit of extra sorting time depending on the ripeness of the apples. Also expect to wait longer before the cider reaches its peak after bottling: it's best to age it for a year or longer.

Preparation
Sort the fruit. Keep in mind that they can be very dark brown and still taste amazing – don't be afraid to break them apart and smell them. Sort out and discard those with visible mould or that smell mouldy. Wash the fruit in cold water.

Crush the fruit. It's good to leave it to pre-macerate for 24 hours or overnight, to extract as much flavour as possible from the skins and to lift the ripe notes and the slightly oxidized feel in the cider. We have pre-macerated for several days and up to 1–2 weeks before pressing with good results. However, remember to stir the top of the crushed pulp so that it doesn't dry out. It's not unusual that it starts to ferment after a day or so. After your desired pre-maceration time, press the fruit pulp and pour the juice into a suitable fermentation vat.

Fermentation

Try to achieve as long a fermentation as possible, rack often (3–4 times) and fermenting a cold temperature.

Sometimes it can be difficult to get the fermentation going when using such ripe fruit, which is why it's a good idea to do a longer pre-maceration. The longer contact with the skin, which is packed with yeast energy, makes it easier for the fermentation to take off.

Bottling, bottle fermenting and ageing

This cider is suitable both as disgorged and un-disgorged. We prefer to not disgorge our ciders from the most complex and oldest trees that we make in this style, but instead let the yeast contribute its body and flavour. But it's also well-suited for disgorging, and you will get a cleaner cider with more over-ripe apple notes. If you have used crab apples, those flavours will become more prominent through disgorging and the cider will be ready to drink sooner.

If you are not disgorging:
approx. 1.003–1.005 SG

If you are disgorging:
1.008–1.010 SG

SWEET CIDER (not alcopop)

Just as with the Swedish/French cider (page 105), dry cider often has a bit of sweetness in it. We would call a wine with 30g (1 oz) of sugar per litre (1¾ pints) a dessert wine, but for cider that is standard for dry cider, at least for French dry cider.

More often than not, our ciders contain 0–5g (0–⅛ oz) of sugar per litre (1¾ pints), bone dry in other words. Sweetness is a sensitive subject in craft cidermaking since so many use it to make the cider taste bigger and more full-bodied. Very sweet cider with various strange colourings and flavourings added to it is more like an alcopop than cider, if you ask us.

But sometimes a little bit of sweetness is very tasty and good for balance and achieving that incredible thirst-quenching quality, especially after a hot, late-summer's day of picking fruit. So, how do you make a sweeter cider that still tastes good? How do you prevent the yeast from consuming all that sugar? Well, it's not easy. Things can go wrong and then you can get bottles exploding in the basement! Meaning that this recipe isn't something that we recommend you start with, but one to try as you get more confident. Keep in mind that you will need bottles that can withstand the high pressure.

Suitable fruit

We think that the apple varieties that are the most 'boring' and don't work as well for dry cider are the best suited for the slightly sweeter style. It's those green and fresh notes in particular that can go well with a bit of sweetness. Good varieties to use are Aroma or Mutsu (aka Crispin). You can also mix in some crab apples if you can find any, to increase the acidity and the structure.

Start with around 100 kg (220 lb) apples. The reason why you need more fruit than in earlier recipes is that you will need two batches or more. If you don't have that many apples, you can use smaller fermentation vats instead. Start by making a pure apple cider: use no other fruits until you have mastered the technique.

Duration

This cider requires more time and experience than the earlier recipes in the book. In addition to the preparation stage, you will need to invest more time in the fermentation stage, so don't squeeze in the cidermaking just before going away on holiday. The time to make the cider varies depending on the temperature but allow at least 2–3 months before it's ready to drink, and ideally longer.

Preparation

Sort and wash the fruit in cold water. Crush the fruit and leave for a quick pre-maceration, approximately 4 hours, or press it straight away to keep the cider as fresh as possible. Divide the juice into two or three 30-litre (6⅔-gallon) fermentation buckets or several smaller demijohns, the classic, rounded glass containers.

Fermentation

This is when things get a bit tricky. To succeed in making a sweet cider without adding enzymes, as in the keeving method (see page 9), or without access to a microfilter, which makes your cider cleaner than Marie Kondo's bookshelf, you will need a cold temperature and patience. When the fermentation has started you have to place the vessels in a cold room, preferably around 8–12°C (46–54°F) or slightly colder, where the cider can ferment slowly and sediment well. A good sedimentation at this stage is key.

Rack the cider often (approximately 4 times before bottling) into new vats so that you continuously remove the gross lees at the bottom. Don't be greedy – remove a lot of the yeast and rack it properly: the fermentation will take a lot longer because of this. You can collect the lees you've removed in a container and leave it to settle, leaving you with a juice that can be reused. This is what we use for our 'Daft Frukt' cider, proper funky stuff. Or wait and let it turn into vinegar.

After each racking, top up with cider from one of the other fermentation vats in order to keep the fresh style of the cider and prevent oxidation.

Blending

You can say that each racking is a blending – that's why you keep the same base cider in different fermentation vats. Make sure to always top up with 'clean' cider that has sedimented well, to avoid doubling up your work.

Bottling, bottle fermenting and ageing

This is absolutely the most sensitive stage. When bottling, you want some fermentation going on, but extremely slowly, and the juice needs to be as clean as possible. Keep an eye on the sugar content, measuring often so that you know it's alive. Aim for it to ferment approximately 1.001 SG per week when it's time for bottling. On the bottling day, put your ear to the vat and listen out for activity. If it's completely quiet, you will have to add more juice that is fermenting to try to get it going again.

Good sugar content when bottling is:
1.013–1.016 SG

You will need to use bottles that can withstand the pressure, bottles specially made for sparkling drinks.

A good way to see if it's okayready to bottle is to take a bottle with a swing top, half-fill it with fermenting cider and leave it by the fireplace (or other warm place) overnight or alternatively for a day or two. If you get a volcano when you open it, it's not ready to be bottled, but if the bubbles stay in the bottle, you can go for it. The longer you age the cider, the better, but wait for a few months to half a year at least before you show it to the world.

112

STEREO THIS IS NOT A CIDER

CIDER IS MADE FROM FRUIT AND
ELSE. IN SWEDEN HOWEVER, IT
ED TO USE UP TO 85% WATER,
NGS AND SUGAR AND STILL
CIDER. WE ASKED OURSELVES
LD A "CIDER" WITH JUST 15%
TE? AND WE GAVE IT A TRY
E RESULT. TO US IT TASTES LIKE
PPLE LEMONADE, IT'S LOW IN
AND HAS JUST A BIT OF TANNIN
E FRUIT PULP (LEFTOVERS
"REAL" CIDER PRODUCTION, TO
GIVE A RICHER FLAVOUR TO
), IT HAS A NICE NATURAL
AND ALMOST NO RESIDUAL
A GREAT DRINK, BUT ONE THING
E. THIS IS NOT A REAL CIDER.

itchy Cider

BELLON

FRUKTSTEREO

FOLK CİDER (made from press leftovers)

This is a recipe inspired by folk beer. It's not difficult to make a sweet cider with lower alcohol content – but how should you go about making a dry cider with less alcohol?

We use an old method that involves using press leftovers. In France we came across a light, lovely drink going by the name piquette, made from the press leftovers from red wine production, water and a few handfuls of sugar. We were told that it was something that vineyard workers used to make to drink during their long working days, since the wines that were produced were to be sold and not drunk by the workers. The fact that the press leftovers were going to be discarded and were therefore free was no bad thing.

After the first pressing of apples there is still a lot of sugar in the leftover pulp, and by adding water the sugar will be extracted along with a lot of flavours and structure – and you can ferment this without any additives. You could describe the result as a light, fresh, tannin-rich cider lemonade with a low alcohol content. Perfect for quenching the thirst on hot summer days or as a lunchtime drink (but be aware that there can still be 2–3% alcohol left, so no heavy machinery after lunch).

Suitable fruit

Use anything that's left over, a proper zero-waste approach. You might just as well use the leftovers as many times as you can before it's time for the compost heap.

Duration

Since you can skip the crushing stage, you will save some time, plus the pressing will be a lot quicker as you only have to press the skin leftovers. So, try to make this alongside 'proper' cider production and you won't have to invest any extra hours. It will require a bit more attention over the weeks it sits with the skin leftovers, with a stir once a day to prevent mould growth, but if you have a good open vat it will be quick to stir. Allow around 2–6 months to get a finished drink; we think that bottled folk cider usually comes into its own quicker than cider made from 100% juice.

Preparation

Folk cider is easiest and best to make alongside standard cider production. Have one or two extra fermentation vats ready, add the press leftovers to them straight away and add water. Think the same as with the orange cider: 20–25% press leftovers in relation to water is good.

Fermenting

Make sure to push down the fruit cap a few times a week. Re-press the press leftovers after 1–3 weeks. It will most likely start to ferment before the second pressing; try to press it while it's still fermenting. This will make the pressing as easy as possible.

After the second pressing, you will still have lot of sediment, so leave the vat in a cool place and rack after a day or so. Keeping in mind that this is actually water, it's better to leave a bit of extra liquid to settle for another day than to get a lot of sediment and gross lees into the new vat.

It is very difficult to measure the sugar content in this type of cider, since the yeast continuously works through the sugar from the skins. Our experiments have ended up at 1–3% alcohol.

Blending

If you want a bit more cider character to your drink, you can just blend it with some cider ... obviously. Leave everything to ferment together for a few SG in that case. This will make the liquid and the juice mates when it comes to flavour, and you will avoid it splitting.

Bottling, bottle fermenting and ageing

Bottle as cleanly as possible. It's difficult to reach the sugar content that is needed for disgorging, plus it's only a good thing if the yeast makes this beverage taste 'more', fuller and bigger.

Good sugar content when bottling is:
approx 1.003 SG

Best aged for a couple of months to half a year to come into its own.

PÉT-NAT WITH PLUMS

Pét-nat using fruit is an idea that we have evolved ever since we once fermented plums and mixed in grapes and apples. It seemed so natural to add new fruit as and when it ripened around us. Pét-nat is the abbreviation used for the French expression 'pétillant-naturel', naturally sparkling wine. Put simply, pét-nat is a sparkling wine where you create the bubbles in the wine by bottling it while it's still fermenting, so that carbon dioxide is created through the continued bottle fermentation; read more about it on page 125.

If you want to mix grapes, apples and raspberries, go ahead. Why not buy fresh pineapple in the supermarket, juice it and mix with apples or pears from the garden? Pét-nat with carrots? This is actually more of a call to action than a recipe – go for it, be creative and don't let anyone tell you that what you are doing is wrong!

Suitable fruit
Any fruit that you can pick from the garden, in the park or from the hedgerows. But for the sake of simplicity we will tell you what we did for our first vintage, Plumenian Rhapsody. This means 25% plums (we used Victoria), 15% red grapes (we used the Rondo variety) and 60% apples (in our case Cortland).

117

Duration

You crush and press in three batches, so you will have to allow for at least three mornings. Then there's post-maceration with plums and grapes, which will need to be checked daily. One morning for bottling, and then your pét-nat will need approximately 6 months resting in the bottle before it reaches its peak.

Preparation

The difficult thing with plums is the stones, but this is also what makes plums so amazing flavour-wise. Without the stones, the drink will become very sweet and clean, with the stones you will get notes of bitter almond. But the stones are incredibly hard, and if you crush them, they will also release some hydrogen cyanide, which isn't particularly good for you. Mash the plums with your hands and leave the pulp to pre-macerate with the stones overnight before pressing.

Press everything together, the stones, pulp and the juice that has been released. Then add a large part of the pulp and the stones back into the juice for a post-maceration for approximately 3 weeks. Stir in the fruit cap every day.

After approximately 2 weeks, press whole, ripe grapes together with the plums that have post-macerated. It's best to do this slowly to retain the colour of the grapes. The reason why we don't post-macerate with the grape skins is to avoid tannins as much as we can. If you like a bit more structure and tannins, you can of course post-macerate with the grapes for a week or so as well. Crush and press the apples a few weeks later and stir this into the juice.

Fermentation

As we write in the fermentation section (see page 53), pears and plums contain some sugar that doesn't ferment. It can therefore be beneficial to wait until you think that the plums and grapes have finished fermenting before mixing in the apples; that way you'll know how much of the sugar won't ferment. Also keep in mind that plums can leave a fairly flighty sediment, so before you add the apples you should place the vat somewhere cold, approximately 10°C (50°F), until the sediment has sunk to the bottom and you can rack into a new vat.

If you want to disgorge, for a cleaner plum taste, you will need to bottle fairly soon after mixing in the apples. In order to prevent the apples causing it to ferment too quickly, rack it as soon as it has started to ferment.

Leave to ferment for around 1 month after adding the apples: the total fermenting time will be around 3 months.

Blending
Since you blend as you go along, it's important to keep a journal. Take care to write down dates, volumes and sugar content to help you remember what you've done, so you can draw conclusions from it.

Bottling, bottle fermenting and ageing
If you have done your job with the racking after the plums and grapes have finished fermenting properly, the bottling will be easier. Try to bottle as cleanly as possible.

If you are not disgorging:
approx. 1.003–1.005 fermentable SG

If you are disgorging:
approx. 1.008–1.010 fermentable SG

THE THEORY BEHIND THE BUBB

This might not be the chapter to read when you've got five bags of ripe fruit in the hallway and just want to get on with making cider. In that case, it's better to wait until things have calmed down and you can sit down in a comfortable chair with a cool cider in your hand, because here we dive deeper into the production of sparkling drinks. We look beyond the usual limits of cider and after reading this theory section you will be able to realize the potential for the drinks you can make yourself.

The most famous, or at least the most widely recognized, sparkling alcoholic drink in the world, is champagne. Of course, champagne has to come from the Champagne region of France but it also needs to meet a range of requirements in regard to production methods and ageing times.

The method used for champagne is called the traditional method, or the champagne method, and involves the following: you make a still wine that is fully fermented. It can be blended with other vintages, matured in oak barrels or treated in other ways. When the wine is bottled, a 'liqueur de tirage' is added, a solution that usually contains wine, sugar, yeast and enzymes to easily trigger a second fermentation in the bottle. One alternative is to add new juice from subsequent years instead, for a more natural product.

The bottle is sealed and left to rest, apart from a regular, gentle shaking, which is done to stimulate the fermentation. The bottle is left to sit on the lees for at least fifteen months for increased complexity and stability. The lees are then moved to the neck of the bottle by rotating the bottle regularly for 4–6 weeks and gradually tilting it so it is upside down. After this the lees can be removed by disgorging. New wine or sugar solution, known as dosage, is added to achieve the required level of sweetness. The process is finished by closing the bottle with a cork and wire cage.

Pét-nat

Even before the glory days of champagne, sparkling wines were produced using various methods. The method that we are especially enthusiastic about, and which inspired our production, is arguably the oldest. It goes by many names, such as ancestrale, rurale and artisanale. Within the natural wine world, the drinks are called pétillant-naturel, pét-nat for short – which is also the term that we tend to use.

The major difference between the champagne method and pét-nat is that, instead of fermenting the wine, ageing it and then adding dosage or juice as in the champagne method, you bottle wine that is still fermenting. To do this, it's important to know the sugar content at the time of bottling, to be sure that the bottles will be able to withstand the pressure that will build up. This means that you will need to decide whether to keep the lees or whether you will disgorge them later on in the process. Everything from 5–50g (⅛–1¾ oz) of sugar per litre (1¾ pints) can work as long as the bottles can withstand the pressure. If you disgorge the lees, you usually top up with the same drink, using a disgorged bottle to top up the others.

Other methods

Another way of making sparkling wine, which is more efficient and allows for more control, is the transfer method. With this you bottle the wine, add liqueur de tirage and leave it to bottle ferment – but after a few months the wine is transferred from the bottles to a large pressurized tank. You usually filter out the lees, add dosage or new wine, and then refill the bottles under pressure. The method is regarded by many as a cheaper way to produce bottle-fermented products, but since the equipment is very expensive it's difficult for a small producer to do – and there is a risk that you lose complexity, and any impact the yeast would have disappears in the filtration.

For an even more efficient production, many producers will skip the bottle fermentation altogether and will instead pressurize the whole vat with fully fermented wine, then add sugar and yeast to trigger a second fermentation that produces carbon dioxide. The carbon dioxide is kept in the vat and the bottles are filled under pressure. This method is usually called the Italian method or the

126

Charmat method and is used for the world-famous prosecco and other simpler sparkling wines with a high level of fruitiness.

The easiest and least exciting way to make sparkling wine is called the injection method and is of course the most cost effective. After the base wine has been produced, the beverage is manipulated to exactly how you want the end result to be. It's filtered and blended, flavourings are added, and the sweetness level is adjusted. After this, you simply inject carbon dioxide, just as for fizzy pop, and bottle the wine under pressure. The bubbles that are formed are usually large, unintegrated and will disappear quickly, just as in fizzy pop.

The regulations in most European countries say that a sparkling wine should have a pressure of 5–6 bars in the bottle. That's about double the pressure of a car tyre. Champagne, crémant, spumante and sekt all sit within this segment. France's pétillant, Italy's frizzante and Germany's spritzig have less pressure and are therefore not allowed to be called sparkling. These are categorized as pearling or semi-sparkling and will have a pressure of 1–2.5 bars, fewer bubbles and are therefore regarded as simpler by some. Since we usually bottle the cider at a lower sugar content and don't disgorge, most of our drinks have a pressure of around 2–2.5 bars.

Maceration with inspiration

As you will have noticed, we work a lot with maceration, both pre-maceration just after the crushing of the fruit and post-maceration once the juice has started to ferment. Post-maceration for us means that we add the fruit pulp and/or other kinds of whole berries to the juice while it ferments. This method of maceration is directly inspired by how some winemakers leave grape skins and sometimes whole grapes to soak in the grape juice.

One example from the wine world is a wine style that has become more common over the last few years, the so-called orange wines. To make these, you let the juice from white grapes, or grapes that are usually pressed directly for white wines, soak together with their crushed skins for a shorter or longer period of time to give the wine more aromas, flavours, tannins and structure. You simply make a white wine as if it was a red wine. Because what makes a red wine red is just the skins that are soaked together with the juice for a period of time. We produce an orange cider that is inspired by this method, among other things, and you can find the recipe on page 100.

Carbonic maceration (macération carbonique)

If whole bunches of grapes, with their stalks, are added to a low-oxygen vat that is pumped full of carbon dioxide, a low-oxygen fermentation will start inside the grapes, which will convert into alcohol and fruity aromas. When the grapes' structure breaks down, a couple of percent of alcohol will have formed and the grapes will release most of their juice because of this. At this stage, or even earlier, the juice is pressed, and the fermentation is continued without stalks, skin and seeds. This method is probably most well-known in Beaujolais in southern Burgundy and is usually called macération carbonique, and nowadays it's used all over the world to make slightly lighter and fruitier wines with less tannins.

Another common technique nowadays is to use some whole bunches or hand-picked grapes together with crushed grapes. This will create an environment where carbonic maceration and standard fermentation can happen simultaneously. Some of the grapes will sit underneath the surface without access to oxygen, while a significant amount of the crushed pulp and the juice will have access to oxygen and will ferment the alcohol the standard way. This method means the pH values are balanced and there is less chance for bacterial and other contamination; at the same time you get some components from the carbonic maceration that will create more texture and balance in the acids than if you don't macerate. This method can of course also be used with fruits other than grapes, something that we like to make the most of when making our drinks. If we mix whole berries and crushed plums into the juice, for example, we can create a natural balance and also slow down the fermentation since not all the sugar is available all the time. Instead more sugar is 'added' during the fermentation process itself as and when the berries burst after the internal fermentation inside the cells.

Flor

From the winemaking world it's also useful to know about flor (which we also write about on page 73), as this can form relatively often when we ferment our fruit drinks. Flor can be described as a film that forms on the surface of the fermenting wine, to protect the wine from oxidation. What happens is that the yeast's cells develop a kind of waxy surface that makes it rise from the bottom to the top, where it forms a film.

Flor can give the drink a more bready, nutty and salty expression; it becomes more complex at the expense of some of the fruitiness. For us, flor is something that you shouldn't be afraid to keep on the surface of your vats, but it will entirely depend on what style you want for your finished drink.

What about sulphur?

Since yeasts are stubborn little things, you might wonder why we don't do as the conventional wine and cider industries do and add sulphur to keep the yeast and a lot of other things in check in order to make more stable and 'clean' products. For us, and others around the world with the same views about keeping it natural, the answer is pretty simple.

We think that the expression and overall experience of the drink is altered significantly when you manipulate it with sulphur. A lot of it comes down to preconceptions about how a product should smell and taste. Additions such as sulphur are one of the reasons why the energy and liveliness in the drink is muted or has disappeared completely. This doesn't have to mean that it smells or tastes of sulphur, as many believe, it's more about how the drink is perceived from a wider perspective. It's more a lack of something exciting in wines that follow a template. By using sulphur, you can create products that taste exactly the same every time you try them. Some like to use a smaller amount of sulphur to minimize the risk of something going wrong. We choose to work completely without sulphur and have the courage to trust the craft completely instead.

The selection in this chapter is based on the fruits we work with the most and that are relatively common. We describe the character we think they possess and how to make the most of them when making cider. But don't feel limited – all fruits are unique and can be used for cider, just in different ways. With curiosity and an appetite for experimenting, anyone can, with limited means, create drinks using fruit and nothing else.

APPLES

For us, it doesn't actually matter what an apple is called or where it comes from. We bite into it – and if it tastes nice and has a good structure and balance, we crush, press and ferment it. We learn more from every new apple we sample. Even though we're not pomologists, our knowledge bank grows with new apple varieties every season.

Size and shape, the colour and structure of the skin, the stalk, the calyx and the interior with core and seeds are all details that distinguish apple varieties from each other. The character and shape of the tree, the leaves and the bloom will also give clues as to what variety it is. Because of things like grafting, rootstock, cross-pollination and clones, identifying the variety isn't always easy. Besides, apples from the same tree can look completely different from one year to another, depending on the weather. For those who are interested, there is a plethora of reference books and apps that can help in identifying apple varieties.

The weather is different every year and this has a significant impact on the final fruit. Whether the start of the spring is warm or cold, the success of bees' pollination early in the season – everything will have an effect on how much fruit there will be in the autumn and its quality. Cold weather means that the fruit will have longer to develop aromas and complexity – as long as it's got enough time to ripen.

One thing to keep in mind is that later varieties, that normally only ripen in November/December at the earliest, are often more structured and complex than early varieties. These later varieties are hardier and can stay on the trees for longer. When they do, more aromas and flavours will develop, and they can therefore give more structure to the cider.

Since we usually pick dessert apples and cooking apples that are relatively neutral in comparison with crab apples and traditional cider apples, it can be a good idea to choose smaller apples with thicker skins, since they will give slightly more tannins and structure than larger fruit. Large apples will, on the other hand, yield more juice.

AROMA

Aroma is a common Swedish variety, first raised at the Balsgård nursery in north-eastern Skåne. The apple is a cross between Ingrid Marie and Filippa, but the result is less aromatic than the two parent varieties, at least in our opinion. The shiny skin is fairly thin in relation to the size of the fruit. Aroma is harvested in early autumn and can be stored for some time, but not too long since the flesh is so porous and juicy.

It is high in acid but apart from this it will give a fairly neutral juice with a short finish. After fermentation, the flavours are still neutral and fruity but lack slightly in depth and length. As a general rule, Aroma won't give any tannins and the body feels a bit meagre and short – it is therefore usually a perfect complement to a lot of other fruit, unless you use a longer maceration, storing, or pick fruit from old trees.

Since Aroma is light in style and mainly apple-fruity in character, we have mostly carried out short macerations to retain that fruitiness. Since the character is so light and neutral, we like to use it in blends, mainly in macerations with berries. This means that the berries give the prominent flavour, but with a lovely freshness from Aroma at the base. In other words, it's a team player of note.

Belle de Boskoop is of Dutch origin. It has become a very popular apple around the cheese mecca of Gouda, because of its versatility in cooking and baking.

The apple ripens very late and can sometimes remain on the trees after the first frost or when the tree has lost all its green leaves and looks like it is done for the season.

Belle de Boskoop has a very hard flesh and a tough, thick skin that is matt and dry.

The apples are relatively large and are well suited for storing. They take on a lot of character from their locality and are therefore very interesting to macerate for slightly longer to extract more flavour and minerality from the skin and core. It results in a complex cider that will improve with ageing.

Belle de Boskoop is a big favourite of ours, since the fruit are large and juicy, as well as being rich in flavour and minerality. If the apple is used straight away the juice is green and crisp, but with storing it will develop a more interesting flavour profile with more ripe orange and red elements.

136

BELLE DE BOSKOOP

BRAMLEY

Bramley, or Bramley's Seedling, originates from a village in Nottinghamshire, England, where you can still view the original tree. Despite it being over 200 years old it still produces a good amount of fruit.

Both the tree and the fruit can be very big and some trees have been known to yield over a tonne of fruit. Because of the fruit's size you will be able to extract a lot of juice, but despite this the flavour has

a good structure and length. Since the trees can grow very big, the roots reach far down into the ground, giving a lot of minerality to the fruit. The skin is green with specks of red and the raw fruit has a green, fresh bite with a good balance due to the naturally high sugar content and, in many cases, the age.

In its home country, Bramley is still the king of the kitchen, where it's used in all kinds of cooking and baking.

The apples keep their high acidity and flavour as their flesh cooks to a purée. We like it mainly because of its minerality and long finish. Another benefit is that each tree yields enormous amounts of fruit and it's therefore easy to get a good volume of juice. The disadvantage is how to get to the fruit that sits high up in the crown.

This apple is therefore most suited to those who like climbing trees.

COX'S ORANGE PIPPIN

Cox's Orange Pippin is one of the more common varieties in the UK and Sweden. The tree is incredibly popular in gardens and in commercial cultivation. It was first grown by the brewer Richard Cox, who is also the man behind Cox's Pomona, which is very different from Cox's Orange Pippin but also common in Sweden. Cox's Orange Pippin is, on the other hand, closely related to Ribston Pippin, which isn't that surprising seeing as it comes from a seed from a Ribston Pippin tree.

The tree is smaller than Ribston Pippin and will in general also produce smaller fruits, which is better for cultivation. In Swedish cultivation it has almost completely taken over from its ancestor Ribston. We find it a bit difficult to understand why these two are competing with each other since we think they are two completely different apples with different characteristics. Orange Pippin has a very good flavour balance – sweet, acidic, nutty and at the same time aromatic. The skin is well suited to shorter pre-macerations, but you can also do longer post-macerations to extract the minerality that can sit in the skin if the trees are older. The fact that the fruits are small can be an advantage for longer macerations since you will get a greater proportion of skin in the crushed pulp.

FILIPPA

Filippa is a common apple tree in Sweden, but because of the uneven ripening of the fruit and the tendency for fruit to fall from the tree as it ripens it's more common in gardens than in commercial cultivation. It's also difficult to store Filippa after harvesting since the skin is thin and even the tiniest bruise or scratch means that the apple will spoil quickly. Even when they ripen normally, they are slightly floury in texture and therefore difficult to press.

These factors means that few growers use Filippa nowadays, but despite the disadvantages it has become a big favourite of ours – because of its lovely tropical notes and the almost honey-sweet balance, which when fermented will give a crisp but simultaneously fruity

and mature expression. After bottle ageing this expression will become even more pronounced.

As with other apples, the character of Filippa varies a lot depending on the age of the tree and where it grows – but in general the apples are large and juicy with a high level of natural sweetness.

On the other hand, we have also picked tiny Filippas with a more concentrated expression. Short maceration is best because of their slightly floury texture. Too long a maceration makes it difficult to press and the flavour will easily become oxidized, almost edging towards caramel.

GRAVENSTEIN

Opinions are split when it comes to this historically very popular apple. Because of the name, many believe it has German origins, but Gravenstein has grown in north Italy and Denmark for a long time. Today, the variety is slowly dying out since many avoid planting the gigantic trees.

Their size makes them difficult to fit into small gardens and impractical for modern cultivation, where trees are required to be more conveniently sized so that they are easy to prune and harvest.

We think it's a shame that Gravenstein is in decline since the large yellow apples are juicy and aromatic, with a fairly intense and powerful finish. There is also a red Gravenstein variety that shares many of its qualities.

One disadvantage is the apple's relatively thin skin, and it should therefore be processed immediately after picking. We use in the same way as other more fragile varieties – a short pre-maceration puts the fruity qualities in focus. When treated in the right way, it's an outstanding apple.

INGRID MARIE

Ingrid Marie is of Danish origin and came into being through a chance cross-breeding between its British ancestors Cox's Orange Pippin and Cox's Pomona. Nowadays the tree is planted across large parts of Sweden, both by fruit growers and homeowners. Ingrid Marie is a robust and hardy apple and has a good balance between sweetness and acidity. The long growing season also gives it highly aromatic notes. The apple is small- to medium-sized, but of course the size can vary from

year to year. Ingrid Marie has a sister named Karin Schneider and they share similar qualities – they both thrive at the Christmas buffet, but Karin is slightly shier in appearance and will blush much redder than her sister.

As a cider, Ingrid Marie does well when mixed with many other types of apples, where its acidic, balanced personality is greatly appreciated. Biting into an Ingrid Marie will bring back cherished childhood memories of crisp and sun-warmed October days and tart

apple pie and will give a similar result in the bottle.

If the trees are getting on in years a bit, the apples will become more minerally and then the cider can be made with a longer pre-maceration. On its own and with a short contact with the skin, there is a chance that Ingrid Marie will only give a simple, very fresh and not that complex cider, but why should that be a problem?

RIBSTON PIPPIN

142

Ribston Pippin is another of our favourite 'British' apples (more recent studies show that it probably originates from Rouen in Normandy). Historically it was widespread across Sweden and it can still be found in some of the gardens and orchards that we pick from. In the UK it is used for cooking and as a dessert.

The trees are medium to large in size and very irregular, with branches that sprawl in all directions. The medium-sized fruit hang on the trees for a long time but they are unpredictable – once they have ripened, they tend to all fall down at once without any warning, so you have to keep an eye on them towards the end of the season. When ripe they are crispy and aromatic with a thick, almost leathery skin that is well suited to

longer macerations. They can also be stored, when they will develop tropical and pear-like aromas and an even more leathery skin.

One big disadvantage, however, is that they often get infested with fungus and rot within, which you won't notice from the outside. This has led to this variety rarely being planted anymore and Cox's Orange Pippin is used instead.

We use Ribston in blends with similar apple varieties and with a slightly longer maceration due to its hardness and because the skin can give added structure.

PEARS

There are thousands of different pear varieties and many of them are wild varieties, just as with apples. Only some of them are regarded as suitable for eating or cooking. Pear trees aren't as common as apple trees in Sweden, and the fruit is also a bit more difficult to process and ferment.

The biggest difference in comparison with apples is not the shape as you might think, as some pears are more or less apple-shaped, but the cellular structure of the flesh which means that pears are juicier than apples. One consequence of this is that they can't remain on the trees for as long as apples, and they aren't as suited to storing either. If you keep them in a cold place and/or a low-oxygen environment it can be done, but there aren't any benefits gained from doing so.

The acidity is also very different from apples. As a general rule, pears contain less acid than apples, and therefore provide a better breeding ground for bacteria and volatile acids during the fermentation process.

Some of the most common eating varieties we use are Alexander Lucas, Conference and Clara Frijs, but we have also come across Moltke, Williams and Beurré Gris, which are common varieties in gardens and old orchards in Skåne.

ALEXANDER LUCAS

Alexander Lucas originally comes from the Loire Valley in France, which back in the day was world famous for its enormous pear plantations brimming with different varieties. The pear is actually not dissimilar to the classic Loire pear Anjou, which got its name from one of the main districts along the river. Historically, there were extensive orchards here, where today mainly grapes are grown.

The name Alexander Lucas comes from the German nursery director who made the discovery. The pears are usually large. The juice is sickly-sweet, but the relatively thick, shiny skin can contribute more flavour to an otherwise rather plain fruit.

This type of pear lends itself very well to experimentation in cidermaking – try short or long maceration (or everything in between), since it hasn't got a lot to contribute otherwise.

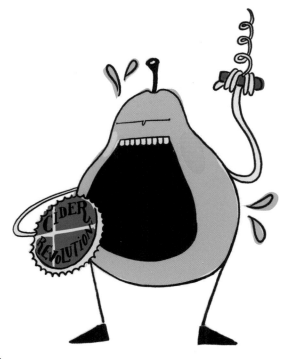

CLARA FRİJS

This Danish pear is the most common pear variety in Sweden and has been growing in our country since the middle of the nineteenth century. The name comes from the wife of the Dane who found the first trees in a forest in south Zealand in Denmark. It is still grown widely in Scandinavia, which is a little surprising since it has a very thin skin and therefore can't be stored for very long.

The flesh is very sweet with a slight freshness and aromatic notes. The fruits are medium-sized and go towards yellow in tone at the relatively early ripening. As with most pear varieties, you can experiment with different maceration times to find what you think works the best. It can smell anything but delicious and fresh during the fermentation but with some patience it can become a lovely fermented juice.

CONFERENCE

Conference became world famous after it won first prize at the British Pear Conference in 1885. The success was instant, and its name a given. Not long after, the first trees came to Sweden; they were first planted at Alnarp and thereafter spread to growers and gardens around the country.

Conference has a long, thin shape and a juicy flesh with a sweet flavour, a fairly common description for cultivated pears. The skin is relatively thin, and often the pears don't have any seeds, which means they can't give much tannin or structure to the cider. Instead, use it to create a bit of volume and blend it with apples or other fruit that can contribute structure and aroma.

BEURRÉ GRIS

Beurré Gris was in the past a fairly common and popular pear and can therefore often be found in older orchards, especially in the countryside in southern Sweden. However, it's not widely grown nowadays and is rarely found in shops, which is a shame. The trees can grow large and produce a lot of fruit, but it ripens at very different stages, which means you have to do several rounds of harvesting. This may be one of the reasons why it's not such a common variety any more.

The pears are often small, the skin grey to green and fairly coarse and rough, which means that you can get a good structure through maceration. The flavour is also interesting and with a certain aromatic quality, which many cultivated pear varieties often lack.

WILLIAMS

A classic pear variety that emerged in the eighteenth century and came to Sweden in the middle of the nineteenth century. The fruit are large and firm and can develop spicy notes when ripe. The pears are often used for distilling in southern Europe; the distilled spirit is called Poire Williams. Our first encounter with Williams was in the form of distilled spirit: it was hard to avoid this noble drink at an Austrian après-ski, served in a shot glass with a preserved chunk of the same grainy and sweet-ish pear.

As with most other pears, Williams can be pressed immediately after harvesting for a neutral juice, or you can give them some time to macerate, when they will develop more spicy character and aromatic notes.

148

QUINCE

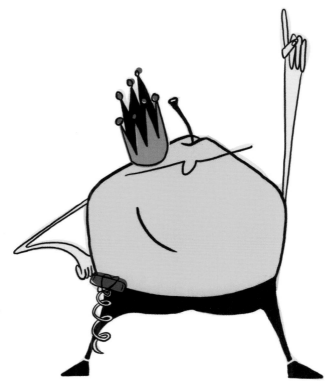

Quince are part of the Rosaceae family, like apples and pears, but are the only species in the genus Cydonia. The fruit looks like a large golden apple or pear, but has very hard and woody flesh that is almost impossible to bite into straight from the tree. Before they ripen, they are small, brown and hairy, but from this cocoon-like fluff a bright yellow fruit will soon emerge, that smells very aromatic and edging towards citrussy.

In Sweden this wonderful fruit isn't very common due to its long growing season that requires a lot of sun and warmth – if you talk about quince in Sweden it is usually flowering quince that is referred to, an ornamental plant that is far from the real deal. You will usually come across proper quince trees in old abandoned orchards around the country or in the garden of someone who is unusually enthusiastic about gardening.

Consider yourself lucky if you can find a tree to pick from, because this is the king of fruit. Just remember to use it in small quantities since its very aromatic character will overpower everything in its vicinity.

PLUMS

Plums belong to the large Prunus genus and come in a range of different varieties with different characters. All plum fruits have a stone or kernel in the centre that shouldn't be eaten. They can range from super sweet and juicy to small and bitter. We love them all for their acidity in combination with sweetness, bitterness and nutty flavours, which are perfectly suited to many of our drinks.

150

Just as with most other fruits that are cultivated, the varieties have been developed to be more edible and user-friendly than their wild ancestors. There is a plethora of subspecies but the most common ones in Sweden and the ones we have come across are the following:

Mirabelle plums (1) are also known as cherry plums since they are similar in size to cherries. Yellow is the most common colour, but they can be anything from light yellow to dark red and everything in between. They are perfect for cooking and baking, with super high levels of acid and a small amount of flesh in relation to the size of the stone, which creates a slightly nutty flavour.

Greengages (2) are round and usually larger than Mirabelle plums. They are often green, dark blue and burgundy variants. They are often known by their French name, Reine Claude. Greengages taste greener and contain a bit more tannins than Mirabelle plums. In addition, they have a higher flesh to stone ratio than their tart friends.

Egg plums (3, 4) are named after their shape. Their proper plum flavour has made them very popular. They can be yellow, red or violet in colour. Many of the most famous and common plums in our older gardens belong to this group. Opal, Victoria and Jubilee are a few celebrities. They have a sweet acidic plum flavour and a lot of flesh and are well suited for cooking and baking – or why not fermenting?

Zwetschge or **quetsche** plums (5) are more oblong and tapered at both ends, with a long, flat stone inside. These varieties have become more common in recent years because of their fine qualities and flavour, which is usually more robust and balanced than in other plums.

Damsons (6) don't belong to the 'noble' plum varieties but they are delicious plums all the same and well suited to drink making. Both the fruit and the trees are usually smaller than the common plums. The flesh is slightly drier and more floury, but the flavour is fantastic, and that's what matters.

In this category we also have to include another favourite that we use in our production, **sloes** (7). These are a subspecies of plums and as you might already know they taste very bitter. However, they become sweeter after the first frost and we use them in smaller amounts in macerations together with apples and pears.

151

5

3

6

GRAPES

Grapes might not be the most common fruit you will come across in domestic gardens in Sweden, or even in countryside orchards – but grapes have actually been grown in Sweden for hundreds of years. In the past, mainly in greenhouses or orangeries, but also in the open air. In recent times, a number of commercial vineyards have appeared and there is also an increased interest among hobby gardeners and enthusiasts.

Since our climate isn't optimal for cultivating traditional southern European grapes, new hardier varieties are mostly being planted. If your neighbour doesn't make use of their grapes, make sure they are being put to good use instead of letting the birds have them. Years with a warm summer and autumn can yield a good crop and the grapes can reach a ripeness that can make drinkable beverages on their own. And if this doesn't happen, we suggest that you use the grapes in macerations with other fruit, just as we recommend doing with other berries and fruit that aren't able to stand on their own.

152

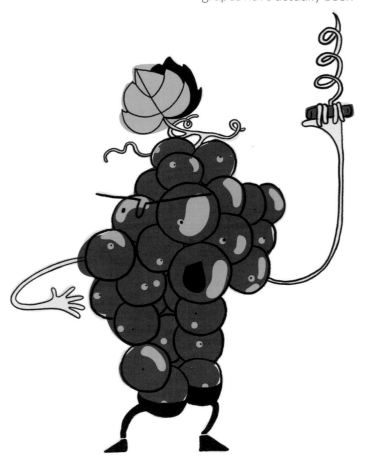

SEA BUCKTHORN

Sea buckthorn is a fantastic berry that grows more or less across the whole northern hemisphere, but primarily in Scandinavia, Russia and China. There seems to be an infinite number of varieties.

They mainly grow in dry, coastal areas, and usually in the form of shrubs with thorny branches.

The thorns make it difficult to pick the berries; the easiest way is to cut or saw off whole branches, place them in the freezer and then shake off the berries. The berries can be anything from pale yellow to dark orange, but they are all jam-packed with vitamin C and sky high in acid. The latter is one of the reasons why we like sea buckthorn and use it in macerations with neutral apple and pear varieties.

Sea buckthorn has tropical notes such as mango and passionfruit, which makes it a wonderful complement to our otherwise classic Scandinavian flavours and aromas.

RHUBARB

For us, ingredients aren't limited to fruit and berries: we like to use other things that grow in many gardens and that have the potential to be made into tasty drinks. Rhubarb is harvested during spring and early summer and it will continue to grow all the way through to late summer. In order to have access to other fruit and berries to mix the rhubarb with, it might be best to use the first harvest for crumbles and in cooking, but the rest of the time it's excellent for making drinks, even when the stalks start to become slightly woody.

Rhubarb is an old medicinal plant which was widely used thousands of years ago in China, although then it was the root that was the desirable part. Later on, the parts above ground also became very popular in kitchens all over the world, and rhubarb wine started to be made.

Many people think that rhubarb is poisonous, and it's true that there are older varieties that are very high in oxalic acid (mainly in the leaves, however), which isn't good in large quantities. There are newer varieties with very low levels of oxalic acid, which tends to decrease as the plant ages.

A bigger problem than oxalic acid for us is that the malic acid in rhubarb is sky high. If you then ferment the sugar off, it will become a bit too much even for acidity fanatics like us, and it can therefore be a good idea to blend the raw juice with something else.

154

OTHER FERMENTABLE FRUITS AND BERRIES

The list of usable fruits and berries is long, but a word of warning before you start fermenting a whole load of blueberries, for example: make sure that you have got to grips with the fermenting process before you start experimenting with ingredients that you have put in a lot of effort to pick.

Currants, cherries, raspberries and strawberries are all interesting to experiment with. Since they have a relatively low sugar content and are high in acid, we recommend blending them with neutral juice from apples and/or pears to achieve a better and more even fermentation. If the fermentation stalls or if all the sugar is consumed, the result can become undrinkable. If only the acids remain, the beverage will not be enjoyable to drink.

To add more tannins or bitterness, wild berries such as rowan berries were used in the past to make the drink more challenging and coarser. This can absolutely be an option if you think the result is too neutral and bland.

Other ingredients to explore are wild berries such as bilberries, lingonberries, cloudberries and crowberries – but they all take a lot of time and effort to pick, so, as we've mentioned, make sure to get to grips with fermenting first.

AFTERWORD

A revolution isn't created by individuals. We were not the first people wanting to change attitudes towards Swedish cider, and neither are we alone in doing this work right now. The opinions we express in this book when it comes to additives and filtering, for example, aren't shared by everyone who works with craft cider – but the fact that people dare to experiment, whichever paths they choose, will lead to an exciting and enlightening diversity. Besides, we think it's a good thing if we in Sweden succeed in creating a varied range of drinks that appeal to people with different taste preferences.

On our relatively short journey we have met many people who have inspired us, who we have exchanged information and experiences with and who have shared our basic principle – to put the fruit first. We were, for example, inspired to start our own production when we drank cider made by Jacques Perritaz at Cidrerie du Vulcain in Switzerland and Eric Bordelet in France.

Riktig Cider is a Swedish importer of craft cider from the classic cider regions. They have campaigned hard to get craft cider sold in Swedish restaurants and directly to consumers and have been a driving force in Svenska Ciderfrämjandet (Swedish Cider Promotion) and in the Swedish Cider Championship, an annual competition for craft cider in Sweden.

Some cidermakers to look out for are Danish Æblerov from Copenhagen and Norwegian Solhøi from Oslo, both of whom have a similar process and outlook to ours. In Sweden there are a number of interesting producers, including Brännland in Umeå and Pomologik in Strängnäs.

We want even more cider buddies, so don't hesitate to join the cider revolution!

INDEX

First published in the United Kingdom in 2021 by Pavilion

43 Great Ormond Street
London
WC1N 3HZ

Copyright © Pavilion Books Company Ltd 2021
© 2019 Mikael Nypelius & Karl Sjöström

First published by Natur & Kultur, Sweden

ISBN 9781911663485

A CIP catalogue record for this book is available from the British Library.

10 9 8 7 6 5 4 3 2 1

Reproduction by JK Morris Production, Sweden
Printed and bound by 1010 Printing International Ltd, China

www.pavilionbooks.com

Graphic design and illustration: Laura Hunter
Publisher: Helen Lewis
Commissioning Editor: Lucy Smith
Design Manager: Laura Russell
Production Controller: Phil Brown